THE ALTAR
OF OUR HEARTS

THE ALTAR
OF OUR HEARTS

GARY WILKERSON

An Expository Devotional on the Psalms

VOLUME 1

Ambassador International
GREENVILLE, SOUTH CAROLINA & BELFAST, NORTHERN IRELAND

www.ambassador-international.com

The Altar of Our Hearts
An Expository Devotional on the Psalms, Volume 1
Gary Wilkerson
©2024 by World Challenge Inc
All rights reserved

ISBN: 978-1-64960-638-9, hardcover
ISBN: 978-1-64960-639-6, paperback
eISBN: 978-1-64960-687-7
Library of Congress Control Number: 2024935427

Cover design by Efrain Garcia
Interior Typesetting by Dentelle Design
Edited by Scott Sawyer and Rachel Chimits

Ambassador International titles may be purchased in bulk for education, business, fundraising, or sales promotional use. For information, please email sales@emeraldhouse.com.

AMBASSADOR INTERNATIONAL
Emerald House
411 University Ridge, Suite B14
Greenville, SC 29601
United States
www.ambassador-international.com

AMBASSADOR BOOKS
The Mount
2 Woodstock Link
Belfast, BT6 8DD
Northern Ireland, United Kingdom
www.ambassadormedia.co.uk

The colophon is a trademark of Ambassador, a Christian publishing company.

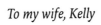
To my wife, Kelly

Table of Contents

Introduction

OVER MY FIVE DECADES OF ministry, I've heard some great preachers. The ones I've loved hearing most are those who approach the podium with their Bible in hand. They open the Scriptures, place an index finger on the page and say, "Let's look at verse one."

Every time I hear those words, my soul stirs. I know I'm about to get a deep dive into my favorite subject: God's Word to His people.

After examining the opening verse, some preachers pause to tell a story or offer an illustration—maybe describing an event from a mission trip, or something a grandchild said, or an anecdote about a historical figure. For the rest of the sermon, they may never return to God's Word. There is a time for stories, illustrations, and life applications; in fact, throughout this book series on the Psalms, I'll tell a few myself. There is no arguing, though, that the greatest, most profound and transformative experience you and I can have together is to experience God's direct word to us. I once heard an elderly preacher say, "When a preacher gets up to preach, he should put his finger on the text and never lift it." That says everything about my driving passion for God's people to know His Word. As you discover for yourself the Lord's amazing character through this series, hopefully you'll sense me nudging, "Look at this amazing text. Take in the powerful truth here. The God of all creation is speaking directly to you."

Jeremiah says it best. "Your words were found, and I ate them, and your words became to me a joy and the delight of my heart, for I am called by your name, O LORD, God of hosts" (Jeremiah 15:16). The Book of Psalms is loaded with memorable meals from beginning to end. In your work life, you may not remember what you had for lunch from day to day, but you'll remember forever what you devoured from this feast of psalms. More than any expensive dinner you could have at a CEO's table, these psalms will transform your life.

The awesome collection of 150 writings that make up the psalter has brought sustenance to God's people over several millennia. It was written over a span of more than 1,000 years by authors as varied as David and Moses, yet its truths are as relevant today as when they were composed. In fact, with some psalms you may think you're reading about current events in the world. One thing is sure, and that is with every psalm you read you'll recognize familiar emotions, deep convictions, and powerful stirrings in your heart.

In each chapter of this volume, we'll put our fingers down on a biblical text and not lift them until we've found life. This treasury in God's Word is meant for deep digging, but most readers flit through it like butterflies, momentarily alighting on a verse and quickly flying away. Many have learned this approach from their pastors' preaching, with Scripture given short shrift. That has contributed to a famine of God's Word in the church. Faithful discipleship requires continual immersion in the Bible, so that when troubled times come, our deep rootedness in God's faithful character will sustain our faith. He is capable of all things in all times, yet if we live off mere emotional highs from stories and illustrations, then the trust we owe Him will wither. I offer this in-depth series on the psalms as a remedy.

So let's put our fingers down together on these texts and begin. We'll partake in the great feast that God has prepared for us in the psalms.

CHAPTER ONE

Psalm 1
Righteous Prosperity

1 Blessed is the man
    who walks not in the counsel of the wicked,
nor stands in the way of sinners,
    nor sits in the seat of scoffers;
2 but his delight is in the law of the Lord,
    and on his law he meditates day and night.
3 He is like a tree
    planted by streams of water
that yields its fruit in its season,
    and its leaf does not wither.
In all that he does, he prospers.
4 The wicked are not so,
    but are like chaff that the wind drives away.
5 Therefore the wicked will not stand in the judgment,
    nor sinners in the congregation of the righteous;
6 for the LORD knows the way of the righteous,
    but the way of the wicked will perish.

A MINISTER FRIEND OF MINE put it best about Psalm 1. He said the
six brief verses that open the book of 150 psalms constitute a roadmap

for a godly life. Psalm 1 begins with a powerful phrase, "Blessed is the man . . . " (Psalm 1:1).

Those four words could not more important to a Christian in any age. Paul told Timothy that in the last days hard times would come upon the earth. "But understand this, that in the last days there will come times of difficulty. For people will be lovers of self, lovers of money, proud, arrogant, abusive, disobedient to their parents, ungrateful, unholy, heartless, unappeasable, slanderous, without self-control, brutal, not loving good, treacherous, reckless, swollen with conceit, lovers of pleasure rather than lovers of God, having the appearance of godliness, but denying its power" (2 Timothy 3:1-5).

Maybe you recognize the current condition of the world in Paul's words. As it turns out, Paul's prophecy here was an echo of the psalmist's words from centuries earlier. Psalm 2 says, "Why do the nations rage and the peoples plot in vain? The kings of the earth set themselves, and the rulers take counsel together, against the LORD and against his Anointed, saying, 'Let us burst their bonds apart and cast away their cords from us'" (Psalm 2:1-3).

Resistance to God has been constant throughout history. The world continually chafes against His way and those who try to live it. The prophet Isaiah spoke of people who actually "call evil good and good evil, who put darkness for light and light for darkness" (Isaiah 5:20). This kind of perversion goes beyond personal morality. When the psalmist asked, "Why do the nations rage?," he echoed the hard history of God's people and the centuries of being attacked, enslaved, brutalized, and abused. The psalmist asked, in essence, "Why do leaders set themselves against God and His way?"

When Psalms 1 and 2 were placed at the beginning of the psalter, they were meant as companion pieces. Together, they form an introduction to all 148 psalms that follow, serving as a framework for the entire collection.

Psalm 1, for its part, speaks mainly of the individual and how to pursue a blessed life. Psalm 2 broadens that scope to take in all of society, bringing a cosmic view to things happening on a global scale.

So how is a blessed life possible despite the continual evil that the world imposes? The psalmist pointed the way from amid his own turbulent day. He began with a bold statement. "Blessed is the man . . ." (Psalm 1:1). Two verses later, he took this further. "In all that he does, he prospers" (Psalm 1:3). In the worst of times, perhaps especially in such times, godly people don't just survive; they prosper.

I hope this rouses a curiosity in you the way it does in me. How is it possible for us to lead a blessed life no matter what may come? Given how messed up the world is, how can it be true of us that "in all that he does, he prospers"? For that matter, what does it mean to be blessed? As I mentioned, the author of Psalm 1 approached this question in an individual, deeply personal way. Today, we hear all kinds of people claim, "I'm blessed!" Some mean their life is problem-free. Others mean their finances are in good shape. A few mean they got a great parking spot at the mall.

None of these are what blessed means in the context of this psalm. The Hebrew meaning of "blessed" here is deeply and profoundly spiritual. To be blessed isn't to prosper materially but to prosper in soul; it speaks of happiness because of a sense of the divine in your life. While we may not always have material goods or decent health or a problem-free life, we can be deeply, profoundly, and immeasurably blessed beyond anything that the world can bestow. This is a profound truth, yet it is within the reach of everyone who calls themselves a follower of Jesus. With that in mind, how is such a blessed life defined, and how is it obtained?

In the opening verse, the psalmist pointed out three ways we can be diverted from a life blessed by God. "Blessed is the man who walks not in the counsel of the wicked, nor stands in the way of sinners, nor sits in the seat of scoffers" (Psalm 1:1). Here is simple, clear direction for how to pursue the blessed life. First of all, we don't listen to the counsel of wicked people. Second, we don't stand with them in their sin. Third, we don't sit around scoffing as they do. These may all sound like similar things, but there is a progression here—or, rather, a regression or descent—in the three steps that the psalmist named.

He used the metaphor of walking, standing, and sitting. Think of these three ways of engaging in evil company as a visible descent. It begins when we walk according to evil advice, entertaining something harmful to our soul. The next step is to stop near it and take it in. The final step is to sit down and settle in its midst, giving ourselves over to it. Consider this descent: Anyone who moves from walking to standing to sitting is gradually lowering themselves. It changes a person's view from high to low.

The psalmist was using a literal scenario to describe a spiritual condition. As we lower ourselves to a temptation of thought, word, or action that we know is wrong. Our perspective changes and so does the condition of our soul. The psalm shows us that to be blessed requires some spiritual vigilance. We have to summon the will to say, "I may be drawn by the things of the world, but I won't let myself be snared by them. I'm going to remove myself from everything that keeps me from the blessed life. I won't purposely walk in evil or stop to take it in or settle down in its midst." This isn't just a matter of willpower; all of us have been humbled by our attempts at self-determination. We know that the process of avoiding evil has to be driven by the empowering grace of God.

We also have to be wise to the temptations that cross our path. Satan never begins by saying, "Hey, take a seat here and start scoffing at God." Instead, he starts with a lesser suggestion like, "What's the harm in walking with these sinners? You don't have to get on the ground and roll around in grime. Just walk with them and satisfy your curiosity. There's no risk in that."

To me, the spiritual snares we face in daily life used to be obvious. There was a time when we clearly knew to steer away from things that we knew were unhealthy to our spiritual life. Today, the snares are so subtle that we're not even aware of them. They've emerged gradually as cultural norms, from what we see on TV shows to what's taught in our education system. Forty years ago, when I was a teenager trying not to be a legalist, I never thought that one day I would be compelled to preach the urgency of putting on spiritual blinders. That's exactly what the psalmist is talking about here.

The blessed life is not about dead religion, not in the least; but it does show us the necessity of continually going to our knees. It also drives us to God's Word. According to the psalmist, this is the second stage of the blessed life. After listing the cautions of verse one, he wrote, "But (the blessed man's) delight is in the law of the LORD, and on his law he meditates day and night" (Psalm 1:2). Instead of walking in the world's evils, we are to place our finger firmly on the pages of Scripture and refuse to lift it until we are reminded of abundant life.

Such an act is a declaration of faith. By removing ourselves from worldly allures, we refuse to be robbed of our spiritual inheritance revealed in God's Word. In its pages we find our delight because everything we read there is wisdom, truth, and sound counsel. The result is that we are empowered to a blessed life. The psalmist attested, "He is like a tree planted by streams of water" (Psalm 1:3). To meditate on God's law is like being a magnificent tree rooted firmly near a life-giving river.

What do you think of when you read the word "meditate"? For many of us, meditation raises images of eastern religion, sitting cross-legged and doing chants. If you're a Christian who accepts the idea of meditation, you may picture acts of serenity like walking through the woods and taking in the glories of creation.

None of this is what "meditate" means in this verse. The Hebrew word used here is actually the same word used for "plot" in Psalm 2:1, "Why do the nations rage and the peoples plot in vain?" In this instance, "meditate" was used in a negative context, meaning to scheme. The energy behind that sort of devious act is the same kind of energy suggested in Psalm 1:2. "But (the blessed man's) delight is in the law of the LORD, and on his law he meditates day and night." Meditation as pictured here is an earnest digging, a determined focus, the kind of dedication that is also required of someone who devises evil plots.

The strongest expression of this Hebrew word also conveyed groaning, like the "groaning too deep for words" that Paul mentioned in Romans 8:23-27. This suggests a powerful, driving longing. If you've ever seen a zookeeper toss meat into a lion's cage, you get the idea. The lion rips into the meat as if it's breaking a monthlong fast.

That's the kind of longing we're to bring to the Bible. When it comes to God's life-giving Word, a lot of Christians are more like butterflies than lions, flitting in and out of the Scriptures. The earnest Christian has a lion's longing cries: "I won't leave this verse until I dig out its deepest meaning. Holy Spirit, help me to understand what You are saying here. What is the truth I need to grasp? What's the significance here for my walk with You? Reveal Your glory in this passage and imprint it on my heart so that it becomes part of me. Help me to memorize this truth so that I never depart from it. May my soul sing it every day."

You may think, "I don't have that kind of longing. I try to summon it from deep within, but it just isn't there. I can't manufacture it; I've tried that and always come up empty. Besides, I know that such self-effort isn't the Lord's way. I want to prosper righteously in Him, and I know I can't by my own doing."

Psalm 1 has great news for you. God is the One Who orchestrates your righteous prosperity. The psalmist declared of the blessed man, "He is like a tree planted by streams of water" (Psalm 1:3). Christ is our living water; all we have to do is be planted near Him and drink from His stream. "Whoever believes in me, as the scripture has said, 'Out of his heart will flow rivers of living water'" (John 7:38).

Planting ourselves by the Lord's stream actually produces delight. When we abide near His living water, we see clearly that His law is life-giving. We thirst for more of it and make it our delight. As we draw on His powerful stream, we see our roots expanding, anchoring us and shooting strength to our branches. Christ's constant stream helps us through not only daily temptations but also through the roughest seasons of life. "(The blessed man) is like a tree planted by streams of water that yields its fruit in its season, and its leaf does not wither" (Psalm 1:3).

What is your soul's condition when you have financial troubles, when your marriage is in a difficult place, when your job is tenuous, when your children struggle in ways that don't seem to have a solution? Are you quick to despair? Do you revisit all your failures? When you see no way out, do you think you deserve defeat, that you're hopeless and no good to anyone much less to God?

When you are planted beside living water, you can draw on His strength to see you through. You'll be reminded of previous trials that the Lord brought you through. You'll remember His faithfulness to show you grace through your hardest times, and you'll find that your load is lightened. In this way, "In all that He does, He prospers." We prosper by knowing His peace despite all outward circumstances; that is how we thrive in life. Most of all, we delight in His Word with an increasing hunger for it. In turn, His life-giving Word generates delight in our soul.

When it comes to prosperity, the psalmist addresses difficult truths. I confess I have always had trouble with Psalm 1:3, "In all that he does, he prospers." Is this statement really true? If so, why aren't our lives glowing successes in every area? I don't know anyone who prospers in everything. That just doesn't line up with my life experiences. As a pastor, I have known plenty of godly saints who pray, love the Lord and take Him at His Word yet who suffer greatly. They resist the false doctrines of "faith teachers" who say that prosperity means laying claim to a bigger house, a nicer car, and abundant wealth. It's true that God loves us and wants us to prosper, but when I consider the effects of the so-called prosperity gospel on people who suffer excruciating trials, that teaching seems as merciless as an attack from Satan. It beats down the godly and discourages them in their pain.

Meanwhile, the godless of this world seem to prosper to no end. "For I was envious of the arrogant when I saw the prosperity of the wicked. For they have no pangs until death; their bodies are fat and sleek. They are not in trouble as others are; they are not stricken like the rest of mankind" (Psalm 73:3-5). Psalm 37 also describes the prosperity of the wicked. It even borrows the imagery of Psalm 1 in its description of a mighty tree spreading its roots. "I have seen a wicked, ruthless man, spreading himself like a green laurel tree" (Psalm 37:35). The prophet Malachi took this even further, pointing out that some evildoers taunt God and escape His judgment. "And now we call the arrogant blessed. Evildoers not only prosper but they put God to the test and they escape" (Malachi 3:15). Meanwhile, as for God's people, the psalmist wrote, "Yet for your sake we are killed all the day long; we are regarded as sheep to be slaughtered" (Psalm 44:22). To me, this doesn't sound like a blessed person who prospers in all that he does.

Passages like these are why we groan and growl to comprehend the Word of God. Life's trials are unrelenting, and for this reason we need roots that are firmly grounded and ever-expanding in Christ's good news. We are driven to find an answer to the question, "What does it really mean to prosper?"

It obviously doesn't mean that temptations will stop coming our way or that every evildoer will be brought to justice in this life. As we ponder these things, we might be tempted to wonder whether God's Word can truly be trusted. I wouldn't blame any suffering Christian for thinking at times, "Is there really any difference between the lives of the wicked and the lives of the godly? Why are people who plot vain things blessed with the things that God promises to His faithful ones?"

You might be tempted to dismiss all of the psalms as "Old Testament" and therefore not a full revelation of God's plan for His people. The apostle Paul contradicted this thinking. He wrote about the sufferings of the righteous with a force equal to that of the psalmist. In fact, he quoted the psalmist directly. "Who shall separate us from the love of Christ? Shall tribulation, or distress, or persecution, or famine, or nakedness, or danger, or sword? As it is written, 'For your sake we are being killed all the day long; we are regarded as sheep to be slaughtered'" (Romans 8:35-36, citing Psalm 44:22).

The tribulations listed by Paul here are serious, yet he wrote them as if they were an expected part of the Christian life. In fact, he seemed to have compiled all the cries of the Old Testament writers. What then was his conclusion about all of these sufferings and injustices? "No, in all these things we are more than conquerors through him who loved us. For I am sure that neither death nor life, nor angels nor rulers, nor things present nor things to come, nor powers, nor height nor depth, nor anything else in all creation, will be able to separate us from the love of God in Christ Jesus our Lord" (Romans 8:37-39).

Here we see the true meaning of righteous prosperity beginning to emerge. Paul then drove home a truth that answers all our cries. "What then shall we say to these things? If God is for us, who can be against us? He who did not spare his own Son but gave him up for us all, how will he not also with him graciously give us all things?" (Romans 8:31-32). Even Jesus was not spared suffering even unto death. According to Paul, as we suffer, we, too, will be given "all things." Here is the ultimate point of his thesis: "For I consider that the sufferings of this present time are not worth comparing with the glory that is to be revealed to us" (Romans 8:18). Paul wrote of an empowering grace that comes only through the cross.

Here is true encouragement for you. When things in your life don't add up, when you're suffering and feel like a lamb being led to slaughter, when prosperity seems like the farthest thing from your reality, you will thrive because you are planted by the river of life that is Christ. Your rootedness in Him provides a continual flow to your hurting soul in all situations.

This is true prosperity, the thriving of a soul in a righteous state despite all circumstances. The psalmist counseled, "Fret not yourself because of evildoers; be not envious of wrongdoers! For they will soon fade like the grass and wither like the green herb" (Psalm 37:1-2). Evildoers will not thrive as we do. It is true that some won't face justice in this lifetime, but their work, life, legacy and soul will fade. Nothing about them will ultimately stand. "In all that he does, he prospers. The wicked are not so, but are like chaff that the wind drives away" (Psalm 1:3-4).

These verses describe the wicked. The people I'm about to describe are not evildoers, but their fate can be like that of the wicked because they've let themselves be deceived. My heart breaks over followers of the so-called prosperity gospel because they have put their faith in a deception. As long as these folks are problem-free, they're happy and content; but when they lose their job or spouse or child or health, their faith can crash, burn and end up in ashes. I often hear them cry, "God isn't faithful. If He were, then where is He right now when I need Him most?" Tragically, they placed their faith not in the Lord but in a doctrine promising things that God never intended. When the winds of life's trials came, every prosperous part of their soul got blown away.

Because they never planted themselves by the true river of life, many end up in the seat of the scornful. They spew bitterness toward God and the church because they feel that they were betrayed. Some even focus their anger on "the blessed man" of Psalm 1, righteous men and women whose souls prosper in genuine ways. Note the regression of those embittered by their deception. They descended from a place of faith to a walk pursuing worldly prosperity and security to a place of bitter scorn. In the end, they have willfully taken their place among the wicked.

The author of Psalm 1 concluded by comparing them with the righteous. "Therefore the wicked will not stand in the judgment, nor sinners in the congregation of the righteous; for the LORD knows the way of the righteous, but the way of the wicked will perish" (Psalm 1:5-6).

Meanwhile, the righteous know the blessed life in full. Over my decades of travel to developing countries, I have met people who don't know where their next meal will come from. Some have to walk miles just to get a small measure of water, if there is any available at all. As I have observed them and heard their joyful songs of praise, I've realized they are clearly blessed beyond most Christians I've met elsewhere in the world. Despite their lack, they possess a great strength of soul because of their confidence in Jesus.

These men and women prosper in righteousness because they have embraced Paul's words, "What then shall we say to these things? If God is for us, who can be against us? . . . how will he not also with him graciously give us all things?" (Romans 8:31-32). God has blessed them with the deepest nourishment of all, filling them with joy and delight that carries them through everything.

Our culture subjects us to multitudes of things that can drive us away from the blessed life. In a surfacy sense, every Christian knows not to walk in the counsel of the wicked nor to stand in the way of sinners nor to sit in the seat of scoffers. As we think of these things, we picture acts of blatant evil being committed. However, the allure of worldly traps can be subtle. This calls for vigilance on our part, and Psalm 1 offers wise counsels about it. If we trust God for the discipline of grace to close our ears to the counsel of the wicked, if we refuse to align our way of life with that of evildoers, if we reject the temptation to scoff after a bitter experience, then we won't have to spend much energy avoiding worldly trappings. We'll find instead that most allurements have disappeared. Temptations will always exist, but our delight will be found elsewhere as we flourish, thrive and prosper in God's righteousness.

If you enjoy this kind of blessed life on earth, how much more will it be true in heaven, in God's literal presence? That will be pure bliss. No more anguishing news of war, injustice, racism and abuse assaulting our senses every day. This is the promise of Psalm 1.

We are not perfect, but we are growing in righteousness. We suffer yet we prosper. Because we are rooted and grounded beside the river of life, the living water that is Christ, then when perilous times come, we'll be able to encourage each other with songs of praise and delight because we know the blessed life.

This is how the psalmist opens to us the doors of this treasury that is the Book of Psalms. He enumerates the ways of blessedness found only in God's magnificent Word.

CHAPTER TWO

Psalm 2

Trusting God in Times of Crisis

1 Why do the nations rage
   and the peoples plot in vain?

2 The kings of the earth set themselves,
   and the rulers take counsel together,
   against the Lord and against his Anointed, saying,

3 "Let us burst their bonds apart
   and cast away their cords from us."

4 He who sits in the heavens laughs;
   the Lord holds them in derision.

5 Then he will speak to them in his wrath,
   and terrify them in his fury, saying,

6 "As for me, I have set my King
   on Zion, my holy hill."

7 I will tell of the decree:
The Lord said to me, "You are my Son;
   today I have begotten you.

8 Ask of me, and I will make the nations your heritage,
   and the ends of the earth your possession.

9 You shall break them with a rod of iron
   and dash them in pieces like a potter's vessel."

10 Now therefore, O kings, be wise;

be warned, O rulers of the earth.

11 Serve the Lord with fear,

and rejoice with trembling.

12 Kiss the Son,

lest he be angry, and you perish in the way,

for his wrath is quickly kindled.

Blessed are all who take refuge in him.

IN PSALM 1, WE READ that steadfast obedience and trust in the Lord leads to a life blessed with peace and assurance. Psalm 2 builds on this, revealing that true comfort and power are available to us even while the world spins in upheaval. As societal chaos creates serious crises, whether through violence, pandemics, racial strife or vicious rage at God, our faith can remain steadfast as we trust that He is faithful through all things.

We don't arrive at such a calming faith casually. In fact, the world's chaos confronts us with a haunting question. "If God is sovereign and all-powerful, ruling and reigning over creation, then why is the whole world in a rage? Why is there all the evil plotting by leaders gone mad? Why is there violence and bloodshed rampant throughout the world? What is behind all the rebellion and rejection of God in our society? Why are multitudes set on casting aside His law?"

I've been in ministry for nearly five decades, and I have never seen a spiritual declension like the one taking place in the world as I write this. I have also never seen Christians so deeply tempted to ask, "Is God even trustworthy at such a time? Our culture is in a death spiral. How could it possibly be true that He holds all things in His hands?" Never have God's people been so troubled and wearied by society's moral decay. In the United States, hearts and minds are vexed over a nation that once respected, honored, and served God but is now determined to wipe Him from its midst. As Christians today look around themselves, they ask the same question that the psalmist asked some three millennia ago: "Why do the nations rage?"

Let's start with the opening word of Psalm 2, "Why?" In Hebrew, this can also be translated as "what." It's as if the psalmist were asking, "What's the deal with so many people questioning God's authority?" The psalmist seems indignant, wondering, "What deception has overtaken people to make them think that they can reject God and yet have any hope of peace? This kind of rebellious mindset only happens in nations that give themselves over to moral depravity."

The psalmist was posing a question to us, and it was answered by Peter in the New Testament. "If by turning the cities of Sodom and Gomorrah to ashes he condemned them to extinction, making them an example of what is going to happen to the ungodly; and if he rescued righteous Lot, greatly distressed by the sensual conduct of the wicked (for as that righteous man lived among them day after day, he was tormenting his righteous soul over their lawless deeds that he saw and heard); then the Lord knows how to rescue the godly from trials, and to keep the unrighteous under punishment until the day of judgment, and especially those who indulge in the lust of defiling passion and despise authority" (2 Peter 2:6-10).

In this passage, Peter explained how God is faithful to His people through the darkest times. At the same time, he reeled off a list of rampant evils that might cause us to despair today. I conclude from this that it's possible to experience a time so dark we can't imagine a way out of it. At such a time, it's easy to feel pessimistic and hopeless. In fact, we may become convinced that our nation is too far gone and totally beyond remedy. When we reach that point in our thinking, all the news that we take in about the world only stresses us more. Peter said this is what happened to godly Lot; he was so overcome by what he saw happening in his day that "he was tormenting his righteous soul over the lawless deeds."

Are these biblical passages mirrors to our own time? Is humankind today dead set against submitting to authority of any kind, whether societal, governmental, or religious? If so, how is it possible for you and me to move forward in faith if we see only darkness around us?

Together, Psalms 1 and 2 form a picture of how to navigate such times. I mentioned in the previous chapter that these two psalms offer a focused framework for every psalm to follow. Psalm 1 deals with rebellion and evil on a personal level, addressing issues of our interior life. It calls us to avoid evil and exhorts us to immerse ourselves in God's Word. Psalm 2 broadens this vision beyond our personal holiness to speak on a larger scale, focusing on the evils of societal, national and global levels.

There is a simple way to think about this pairing of the two opening psalms. While Psalm 1 deals with the Word, Psalm 2 deals with the world. Interestingly, if we get Psalm 1 right and address issues of the heart, we'll be prepared to deal with the outer chaos laid out in Psalm 2. In other words, immersion in God's Word sets our heart on a right trajectory to face the world's difficulties. No matter what kind of storm may rage around us, it is possible to walk boldly with confidence and unquenchable faith. This doesn't come from reading good books by our favorite godly authors; it comes only from trusting in God's Word. To delight in His Word is to have confidence to face any situation.

Do you live in fear? Do you spend sleepless nights worrying about your children? Do you go over your finances repeatedly, trying to make them add up? Digging into God's Word won't make your problems disappear, but your spirit doesn't have to be troubled. You can know real help through the Lord's assuring presence. You may be troubled by the world's chaos, but because Christ is with you in all things, you won't be overcome.

When the psalmist asked, "Why do the nations rage?," he wasn't just talking about one nation. The psalmist's question wasn't about a single nation such as ours or about communist nations or godless, heathen nations. He was speaking of all nations. In this psalm, every nation seemed infuriated at God. This included not just all nations but all peoples. "Why do the nations rage and the peoples plot in vain?" (Psalm 2:1).

As Christians, we tend to point a finger at politicians and say, "Our leaders are so ungodly." The truth is that in democratic societies where we're able to vote for who will lead us, our elected leaders are just an extension of ourselves. They don't comprise our government; they merely represent us in a system of self-government. So in a very real sense, we get what we vote for. You might even say that we get what we deserve. Passages in the Old Testament talk about this, where God's people clamored for a priest or ruler who would tell them what they wanted to hear instead of the path that God prescribed for them.

Note what the psalmist said about the leaders of nations. "The kings of the earth set themselves, and the rulers take counsel together" (Psalm 2:2). The word "set" here means to take a stand, suggesting immovability. These leaders opposed God, plotting "against the Lord and against his Anointed" (Psalm 2:2).

Verse two mentions not only kings but rulers. Applying this to our own day, "rulers" may signify policymakers like judges and lawyers who set agendas for governance. The rulers mentioned by the psalmist shared their counsel with the aim of diminishing or rejecting God's righteous ways. Today, we see something similar as rulers set themselves against the Lord with regulations and mandates that limit religious freedom or even institute evil.

This same verse mentions an anointed one whom the world opposes. Who is this? The psalmist's audience would know this to be King David or another divinely appointed monarch, God's chosen person to rule sovereignly over His people. Most biblical scholars agree that the reference to 'Anointed' here also points to Jesus in a prophetic foreshadowing. Why would people oppose Christ? We find the answer in our own culture. Today, much of the world points to religion as the cause of their problems and wants to diminish its presence in their lives. Some nations look to rid themselves of all public mention of God and limit faith to private expression. "Let us burst their bonds apart and cast away their cords from us" (Psalm 2:3). The picture here is of someone trying to break free from a terrible bondage. What is underneath that desire, however, is a lust to be free of all restraints that only begin with God's law.

The Lord will have none of this. To come against Him in these ways, according to the psalmist, is vanity; "the peoples plot in vain." The message is clear: You may set yourself against God but you can't win. You may be a powerful leader ruling over millions or even commanding the world's greatest military; but if you try to stand against the Lord, you'll find yourself flat on your face, utterly bereft of power or authority.

The New Testament's parallel to this is clear. "For truly in this city there were gathered together against your holy servant Jesus, whom you anointed, both Herod and Pontius Pilate, along with the Gentiles and the peoples of Israel" (Acts 4:27). From the time Jesus was born until the cross, there was never a time the rulers of the land weren't plotting against God. The Lord's plan would not fail, however; His sovereign voice determined how things would go. Against all the worldly forces that tried to thwart

Jesus, God preserved our future hope, which was accomplished in Christ's victory on the cross.

A great deception is embedded in the world's cries to break free from the chains of bondage. This deception claims that God's law is oppressive, holding down humans from their potential. The opposite is true; His law brings freedom. It is sin that brings about bondage. Paul summed up these truths in one concise verse. "For the law of the Spirit of life has set you free in Christ Jesus from the law of sin and death" (Romans 8:2).

Here is good news: The whole world may rage, but God will have His turn. However terribly the world may rage, God endures patiently. Then, at a time of His choosing, He moves in, saying, "Now I am going to speak. I will have my rule." What is His response to all the clamoring voices that oppose Him? The psalmist wrote, "He who sits in the heavens laughs" (Psalm 2:4).

God's laughter over the nations isn't that of amusement. It is laughter of ridicule. "The Lord holds them in derision" (Psalm 2:4). The thought of someone overthrowing God is ludicrous. He simply laughs at the vanity of such plotting. Note the word "sits" in this verse. High above all human scheming, God sits in sovereign power. What a powerful contrast to those who sit in the lowly seat of the scornful and who plot and plan against Him. As the world rages, the Lord doesn't pace around worried, anxious or stressed. He simply sits. This image serves to reassure every righteous person who frets over the chaos swirling throughout the world. The psalmist advised, in essence, "Don't lose your trusting heart. God sits over and above it all."

When verse four says God "holds them," meaning the nations, we picture all the world's nations in His grasp. This isn't necessarily a threatening image. In fact, allowing the nations to rage implies God's patience and mercy. He is all-powerful, yet He doesn't instantly destroy the wicked. In fact, as I imagine God "holding" the nations, I picture a football coach grabbing the shoulder pads of a player who has made a foolish play. The coach gets in the player's face and passionately corrects his mistake. "You know that's no way to run the play," I hear him shouting. "If you keep doing that, you'll fail every time. I've shown you the way to do it so that it will work for you."

"Then he will speak to them in his wrath, and terrify them in his fury" (Psalm 2:5). Few people today, including Christians, want to hear about a God Who speaks in wrath and fury. "That's the Old Testament God," they claim, as if the Lord's character suddenly transformed from one testament to the other. God does have wrath, and it does come, as we see especially in the book of Revelation. However, if you reread verse five or indeed the whole of Psalm 2, you won't find a single word of hatred in it. On the contrary, it conveys a patient, enduring mercy that becomes ever clearer as the psalm unfolds.

When the Lord speaks in fury and wrath, the world falls silent. That is the effect of His holy voice speaking truth with power and undeniable authority. One reason the world falls silent is because its power is revealed as empty and vain. God's Word, by contrast, reveals His omnipotence. What He declares comes to pass.

I love the next phrase, which begins with God saying, "As for me . . ." In other words, "You've had your turn to speak. Now you're going to hear from Me." The nations had raged, the peoples had plotted, and kings and rulers had counseled together against the Lord and His anointed. God responded with one simple sentence. "As for me, I have set my King on Zion, my holy hill" (Psalm 2:6). What does this sentence mean? It means that God had positioned Jesus in His rightful place as ruler over all creation. When this psalm was written, Israel had an earthly king, but this verse prophesied the all-encompassing reign of Christ that was to come. Jesus was set, immovable and possessing all authority, as a sovereign ruler over all nations and peoples.

According to scholars, Psalm 2 was known as the nation's coronation song. Psalm 2 was invoked and quoted whenever kings were installed to rule over the people. When David was crowned king, a peace came over the land. The nation had been troubled because of Saul's conflict with David while the mighty Philistine army threatened. The people's trepidation grew even greater after Saul lost a battle and killed himself. Their fears began to dissipate, however, when David was crowned on Mount Zion. This brought a sense of stability to the nation, and the people began to trust again. When they beheld their new king, they knew God had established a righteous rule.

This serves as an image of the great peace available to us today. Jesus is established as rightful king and authority, reigning perfectly no matter how people may plot and rage. Nations may come against Him to try to diminish His rule, but God answers simply, "I have set My king on Zion, My holy hill."

"I will tell of the decree: The LORD said to me, 'You are my Son; today I have begotten you'" (Psalm 2:7). God didn't select some earthly king or charismatic leader to reign. He set His only begotten Son in authority to bring perfect rule over all things. The Father was saying in essence, "There is only one who will rule in perfect justice, power and peace; and that is my beloved Son."

God then addressed His Son. "Ask of me, and I will make the nations your heritage, and the ends of the earth your possession" (Psalm 2:8). God has placed all things under the authority of Jesus, His anointed. For this reason alone, we don't need to fear the raging of nations no matter how fierce it sounds. All things belong to our ruler; everything is in His possession. Although the world's raging may worsen over time, we can trust that Jesus' reign over all things remains perfect.

After this peaceful reassurance in verse eight, a harsher image follows. "You shall break them with a rod of iron and dash them in pieces like a potter's vessel" (Psalm 2:9). This verse addresses every anxious Christian today who wonders why God allows evil to continue. In chaotic times of rampant evil, some Christians accuse God, "You've allowed this to go on for too long. Nations all over the world are going downhill fast. Lord, why didn't You put a stop to all the raging long ago? Why aren't You doing anything about it now? It's having an effect on all of us. We're losing trust as we watch evil take power, good things be destroyed and Your name disappear from the world. How can You sit by as wickedness rules the day?"

The answer is simple: We know that a day of righteous judgement is coming. When that time arrives, God will say, "Enough is enough," and He will dash to pieces everything coming against Him.

Even as that day of judgment approaches, however, God extends His mercy to the sinful. He stirred the psalmist to issue a grace-filled warning to the wicked. "Now therefore, O kings, be wise; be warned, O rulers of the earth" (Psalm 2:10). Like the furious football coach shouting at his foolish player, God speaks to the raging nations, "Be smart about this. Wake up from what you're doing." As a minister of God, I find Psalm 2 to be a helpful reference point while societies all over the world decline.

True to His character, God is holding off judgment, remaining patient with evildoers. "The Lord is not slow to fulfill his promise as some count slowness, but is patient toward you, not wishing that any should perish, but that all should reach repentance" (2 Peter 3:9). In this verse, Peter presented a picture of undeniable tenderness, describing the vast reach of God's amazing grace. In our own heart of hearts, we may be tempted to wish destruction on those who oppose God and the church, but He faithfully extends grace to all.

This presents us with a further difficult truth about God's grace toward evildoers. His patience is our mandate to reach them with the gospel. When He says, "All should reach repentance," whom do you think are the main messengers of that grace? It's His church. In times like these, we want to take on the yoke of prophets and preach God's righteousness to a raging society. However, as Psalm 2 shows, God's warning to an unrestrained world always includes an appeal to saving, redeeming grace. He sends us forth with a message to unredeemed millions: "Today is a day of mercy and grace, but one day God is going to speak to you in wrath. So hear His voice today, and 'Serve the LORD with fear, and rejoice with trembling.'" In the very psalm that describes God's fury and wrath, He calls out with the voice of a tender Father to kings, presidents, rulers, and leaders to repent and serve Him with holy fear, reverence, and awe-filled joy.

That, in essence, is the meaning behind the strange phrase, "Serve the Lord with fear, and rejoice with trembling." How is it possible to "rejoice with trembling"? That sounds like a contradiction. A healthy-minded Christian knows, however, that awe-filled reverence leads to peace and happiness and not to resentful fear. When I consider God's majesty and holiness, I fall to my knees in humility. Likewise, when I consider His merciful, long-suffering love, I am filled with joy and peace. So even as I honor God with all due reverence, I also want to let loose with a shout of joyful gratitude to Him. These things go hand in hand. Only the religiously rigid resist the joy that comes from knowing God's mercy.

The churches that I attended as a young person could be horribly rules-based with manmade standards, but today the opposite seems to be happening in churches in an equally unhealthy way. A lot of Christians are far too casual about their reverence for God. They don't seem to know that He is high and holy as well as near and intimate to us, and He is therefore not to be mocked. This doesn't mean we take on a somberness that's more about virtue-signaling than a genuine response of the heart. If we truly know both His awesome holiness and His loving, tender friendship, we'll honor Him in every way He deserves with both reverential awe and joyful thanksgiving.

Finally, the psalmist instructs, "Kiss the Son." This command suggests an act of affection and appreciation yet also humility. There is nothing casual about obeying his command to kiss the Son. On the one hand, it signifies love and loyalty; on the other, it suggests laying down all self-sufficiency, pride, and rebelliousness. The next phrase confirms this with an additional warning: "lest he be angry, and you perish in the way, for his wrath is quickly kindled" (Psalm 2:12). The use of the word "perish" here echoes the warning of Psalm 1, "For the LORD knows the way of the righteous, but the way of the wicked will perish" (Psalm 1:6).

Both Psalm 1 and 2 are also marked by the word "way." Again, we see them working together to point the way to a blessed life while also revealing how such a life can be derailed. While Psalm 1 opens by addressing the blessed life, Psalm 2 closes with it. The psalmist's final verse reads, "Blessed are all who take refuge in him" (Psalm 2:12).

The King James translates this verse as "Blessed are all they who put their trust in him." Given the context of Psalm 2, this verse could also be read as "all who take refuge in Him in times of crisis." You may say, "Well, wouldn't it be better if God just eliminated the crisis?" No, that is not the case. In our times of challenge when chaos rages beyond our resources to handle it, we behold God's goodness, greatness, and mercy as never before. As we turn to Him with our trust, we find Him faithful in ways we didn't know possible. This is how we learn the depths of the blessed life.

You may wish not to have to live in a time of crisis, but in such times, the Lord is shaping a people who will serve Him in fear, reverence, and joy. By trusting Him amid chaos, we learn not be stressed, worried, or anxious. Instead, we become beacons of hope when there is no hope other than the Gospel. This draws the unsaved to us. When we stand assured amid terrible chaos, people will approach us asking, "How can you have such peace right now? Things are falling apart. Nobody knows for sure what's going to happen. I'm scared for my family, my finances and my kids' future, yet you don't seem worried at all. How did you come upon this inner peace?"

If we heed the counsel of Psalm 1 to meditate on God's Word day and night, we will be able to face the tribulations of Psalm 2 without being overcome. We will be empowered to stand as pillars of peace in raging storms. We will not be anxious or fearful because we will draw on the living water that nourishes us. As the world trembles, frozen in fear, we will move forward in faith knowing that God's anointed holds everything in His hands. We will carry His message of repentance, mercy, and hope to a waiting world. This is the amazing, all-encompassing framework for the Book of Psalms.

CHAPTER THREE

Psalm 3

It May Look Like I'm Surrounded

1 O Lord, how many are my foes!

Many are rising against me;

2 many are saying of my soul,

"There is no salvation for him in God." Selah

3 But you, O Lord, are a shield about me,

my glory, and the lifter of my head.

4 I cried aloud to the Lord,

and he answered me from his holy hill. Selah

5 I lay down and slept;

I woke again, for the Lord sustained me.

6 I will not be afraid of many thousands of people

who have set themselves against me all around.

7 Arise, O Lord!

Save me, O my God!

For you strike all my enemies on the cheek;

you break the teeth of the wicked.

8 Salvation belongs to the LORD;

your blessing be on your people! Selah

THE BOOK OF PSALMS SPEAKS to every culture in every era, including the present hour. Psalm 3 in particular shows us hope, power, and deliverance for all the crises we find ourselves facing today.

In Psalm 1, we read of a man's temptation on a personal level. He was advised not to walk in the way of the wicked nor to stand with sinners nor to take a seat with the scornful. Psalm 2 broadened this picture to show God's people facing global or societal trials. Turmoil and chaos had overtaken the land, with people and nations raging against the Lord.

This brings us to Psalm 3. Here the writer addressed a completely different level. The writer was David, and he spoke of a painful chapter in his life. The header that appears above this psalm reads, "A Psalm of David, when he fled from Absalom his son." This psalm isn't about personal temptation or societal chaos; rather, it addresses a crisis on an internal level. By internal I mean not only King David's state of heart and mind but also the nation he governed and the family he led. What was David's internal issue? A revolt had taken place. It was coup led not by some ambitious adviser or military general but by David's own son Absalom. For David, it was a horrifying and harrowing development, affecting his life in every possible realm.

What strikes us first about this psalm is David's openness and honesty in detailing a shameful episode for his family. I am continually astounded by the honesty of the Bible's writers. In this psalm, David spoke from an episode that carried great anguish and heartache. The context is out in the open at the very beginning, with the header telling us David was forced to flee from his own son. We can assume the whole nation knew what David was talking about in this very public psalm. David's declaration was akin to you or me leading off a conversation with "My business failed," or "My spouse had an affair," or "My child has a drug problem." Most of us would find it embarrassing or shameful to publicly proclaim these things. In fact, we would probably work hard to keep such things private.

I wonder why we work so hard to avoid dealing with our difficult realities. It's clearly because such things cause us great pain and suffering. Once we face them, we want to put them behind us as quickly as possible. When David penned this psalm, he was running from his own problems; we know this from the background provided in other biblical passages. I think it's worth examining what inspired the biblical writers to be so open about human problems, including their own. One answer, I believe, is that God wants us to be honest with ourselves. He wants us freed up to say, "I'm in a place of trouble. I am so overwhelmed and anguished by my problem that all I want to do is flee."

The honesty in Psalm 3 blesses me as a pastor because I believe it models what the church should be doing. For Christ's church to thrive in good spiritual health, we have to be honest with ourselves, with each other, and most importantly with God. His Word says again and again that He hears our cries. This teaches us not to be ashamed of our troubles or shortcomings. His Word also encourages us to be open about our heart's condition, including our struggles. As His people, we are not to put on masks to cover up the hurts and pains we're going through.

The honesty of Psalm 3 also teaches us that the beginning of a person's story doesn't indicate how it will end. This is an immutable truth for those who follow Jesus. When David said he had to flee from his son, we have an inkling that this would not be how the story ends.

Right now, you may describe your story as one of brokenness, heartache and pain. It may look as though you're surrounded by troubles, trials, and tribulations, and like David, you struggle internally, too. Maybe your spouse has had an affair. Maybe your business has failed. Maybe your child has a substance addiction. This psalm gives us hope and peace about our most excruciating trials.

The context of this psalm is one of extreme turmoil that began in David's family. David's tribulation started when his son Amnon raped his half-sister Tamar. Her brother Absalom responded by killing Amnon. Absalom's terrible act was a vengeance killing, and he was furious with his father because David hadn't done anything about the rape. David had favored Amnon too much and was unwilling to act justly about the rape. All in all, it was a sorry episode in the royal family. After the murder, Absalom fled the land, setting into motion the wheels of a massive revolt. He spent three years plotting how he could overthrow his father. During that period, he gathered to his side more and more supporters, including troops to wage an attack on David. The book of Samuel tells us, "The conspiracy grew strong, and the people with Absalom kept increasing" (2 Samuel 15:12).

David surely was overcome by all of this. His beloved child had just been murdered by another son. Now Absalom plotted to unseat David, removing from his life not just the throne but also God's promises about a family heritage and Israel's future. Meanwhile, more and more of David's people turned against him, pledging loyalty to Absalom. On every side, it seemed, David was surrounded by pain, grief, sorrow, and a growing fear for his life. This horrible setup led him to open Psalm 3 with his own anguished cry. "O LORD, how many are my foes! Many are rising against me" (Psalm 3:1). In that moment, David did not think to fight. The book of Second Samuel unfolds how David's world was falling apart. First came the news of Absalom's power and coming attack. "And a messenger came to David, saying, 'The hearts of the men of Israel have gone after Absalom.' Then David said to all his servants who were with him at Jerusalem, 'Arise, and let us flee, or else there will be no escape for us from Absalom. Go quickly, lest he overtake us quickly and bring down ruin on us and strike the city with the edge of the sword'" (2 Samuel 15:13-14).

Next, David thought he shouldn't bring the treasured ark of the covenant with him. "Then the king said to Zadok, 'Carry the ark of God back into the city. If I find favor in the eyes of the LORD, he will bring me back and let me see both it and his dwelling place. But if he says, "I have no pleasure in you," behold, here I am, let him do to me what seems good to him'" (2 Samuel 15:25-26).

David was overcome by all his mounting losses. I find the image of him leaving town to be heartrending. "But David went up the ascent of the Mount of Olives, weeping as he went, barefoot and with his head covered. And all the people who were with him covered their heads, and they went up, weeping as they went" (2 Samuel 15:30).

David was driven from everything God had given him. He left behind his home, his family, the position God gave him and the nation he governed with honor and reverence. Meanwhile, evil counselors had captured Absalom's ear, filling him with wicked plotting. All these things added up to another grief for David on top of the rape of his daughter Tamar and the loss of his son Amnon. David could only have been in a state of shock as he left the city and ascended the Mount of Olives. All he could do was weep and cover his head.

David's actions exemplify what many of us do when we face overwhelming sufferings. If you've suffered a broken marriage, you've felt losses in addition to the sacred relationship you once cherished. Your breakup may have involved children and perhaps financial devastation as a result. It's likely your psyche was affected, causing you to doubt God's promises of a family and bright future.

Alternatively, perhaps you struggle because of a long period of physical suffering. Maybe you have a chronic physical condition that causes you endless pain. Maybe your mind is assailed with fear and anguish, causing emotional problems that affect your relationships.

Whatever your suffering is, in the midst of it, you may feel tempted to turn to unhealthy escapes or to old habits that once bound you in addiction.

I've known many Christians whose trials came one after another, and others whose trials piled upon them all at once. When David wrote, "O LORD, how many are my foes! Many are rising against me" (Psalm 1:1), he was talking about several trials that happened at one time. With this opening verse, David might have meant one of two things: Either many people were attacking him on a single front, or he was being attacked on many fronts. Whenever our trials pile up, we can be driven to near-despair. Some of us may grow paranoid, our thoughts running wild about worst-case scenarios. We grow panicked over what may happen to us.

Even for Christians whose thoughts remain sound, an avalanche of problems crashing down at once can seem like too much to try fighting. If they had just one problem, they could face it reasonably, but a constant increase that's beyond their ability troubles the soul. They spend every waking hour preoccupied with problems, unable to shake their anxieties and fears. Despite their best intentions, like David they turn to flight instead of fight.

As I've grown older, I have found that griefs and pains can accumulate over the years. The pain from one trial may subside, but a residue remains and gets added to the next trial. Our sorrowful experiences, even when they're behind us, can get compounded in our soul. We may be unaware of this, so that when our next trial comes, old anxieties arise and add to our stress.

Years ago, my wife and I endured a prolonged trial after one of our sons spiraled into an addiction that led to homelessness. He was a teenager when he first tried marijuana. We knew what was happening, and our talks with him had no effect. My wife, Kelly, and I pleaded with God to free our son from what soon became a habit, but things only got worse. Our son no longer listened to us, so we doubled down on our prayer efforts. Next, we learned he had begun using pills. Distraught, we started fasting for him each week. Again, there was no answer to our desperate pleas. Soon our son stopped coming home. We found out he wasn't staying at friends' houses but that he had become homeless, living on the streets. That's when he started using heroin.

At that point, Kelly and I were utterly beyond ourselves. We wept through many nights, unable to sleep and ending up driving down dark streets looking for our boy. Our prayers not only went unanswered, which was a hardship in itself, but the more we prayed the worse the situation became. Eventually, our son's very life teetered on the edge.

Thank God, that was not how the story ended. Jesus knew the ending all along, even if we didn't. Our son got saved, and his turnaround was nothing short of a miracle. As I write this, he has been clean and sober for over seven years and has a lovely family with two kids who are the delight of their grandparents. We are proud of our son, and we've never been more thankful to the Lord for His goodness and mercy to us.

I've never doubted God more than during those years of travail. He seemed too far above our anguish to hear our prayers, detached from our grueling, gut-wrenching reality. I was full of anger at Him, sometimes enraged. After all, I had spent my life testifying to His faithfulness, yet when my greatest time of need came, I sensed no trace of His presence at all. Like many parents, Kelly and I never lost hope, but my faith took a beating. My wife and I knew what it was like to experience life's greatest pain from within our household.

It is true that sometimes those closest to us cause us the greatest pain, almost like a Judas kiss. A particular kind of pain can happen in relationships of intimate trust such as marriage. It can also happen in a church, where another kind of intimate trust is built. As a pastor, I remember being deeply wounded by a trusted colleague. I had always believed everyone intends to be kind, but my belief ended up hindering me when it came to facing this colleague's betrayal. The experience launched in me God's instruction on how to do warfare with battles that are insidious rather than obvious. We have to accept that even in life's toughest trials, the greater battle is always with principalities and powers that attack our mind and soul. These are our most vulnerable areas during times of great struggle.

David faced this kind of insidiousness during his trial with Absalom. Absalom was turning people against him, and eventually David had to flee the glorious city he had faithfully defended against the nation's enemies. Ironically, the people David protected made cruel judgments against the leader they once admired and trusted. Think of how this impacted David. It obviously weighed heavily on his mind as he wrote, "many are saying of my soul, 'There is no salvation for him in God'" (Psalm 3:2).

There is that word again: "many." Interestingly, David used it three times in the first thirteen words of this psalm. He seemed to be saying, "Trials and enemies surround me—many, many, many of them—and they are rising up against me." He used the language of a battle-tested soldier, a mighty warrior who could handle himself in any conflict. However, we sense David's deepest wounds came when others spoke against him, especially those closest to him. He loved the people he governed and protected; he loved the soldiers he led into battle, and he especially loved his large family. That included even Absalom, despite the fury that David felt over his son's murderous acts and traitorous insurrection.

Something is very telling in David's phrase " . . . many are saying of my soul." People weren't attacking David over his behavior but were making a judgment about his soul. Often our greatest strength is our character, and David's was under assault. He wrote awesome songs of worship which were sung by the people, but now those same reverent voices said he was so far gone that he was beyond God's power to save. David was so low in spirit that he might have started to believe this. Hanging his head in a darkened state on the outskirts of town, David may have thought, "Look at me running away without knowing where I'm going. What has happened to the promises of God in my life? I am at my lowest, and yet He is nowhere in sight. Maybe everyone is right; I have no idea where my life will end up. Can I still be saved?"

Scripture's narrative of David's life suggests his troubles began when this mighty warrior let down his guard and followed a temptation of the flesh. David was built as a warrior meant for battle and to fight valiantly for the kingdom of God. His trouble started when he took a break from literal battle and went home for some rest. One day he was strolling on the roof of his palace when he looked down and saw a woman bathing across the way. When David's eyes landed on Bathsheba, he lusted after her. He must have been in a lackadaisical frame of mind because he lowered his spiritual guard and followed his temptation through. David sent for this married woman and slept with her, and she ended up pregnant.

Things grew worse from there. Bathsheba's husband, Uriah, was one of David's top soldiers. To cover up his sin, David tried to get Uriah to sleep with Bathsheba so that when the baby was born, Uriah would believe it was his own. Instead, Uriah followed a common soldier's conviction: He refused the luxury of sleeping with his wife while his fellow soldiers were dying on the front lines. Desperate, David ended up orchestrating a murder. He sent Uriah back to the front lines carrying orders that ensured Uriah would be killed.

David's unthinkable behavior was confronted by the prophet Nathan, and David had to live with the stain of sin on his life ever afterward. Amid the crisis David described in Psalm 3, with crowds turning against him to follow Absalom, David might have thought he was finally receiving judgment for his previous sins as people cried, "There is no salvation for him in God" (Psalm 3:2).

Have you ever been in the same downcast, despairing state of mind as David's? If you struggle with a habitual sin—whether anger or lust or the like—at times you've probably thought, "It's useless. I've never been able to beat this. I'm beyond all help." You have absorbed the accusations of the devil or the judgments that you suspect others make of you. At that point, you become your own worst enemy. Now the voice you hear in your head is not that of others but your own. "They're right about me. There is no hope for me in God. I'm beyond saving." This is precisely where Satan wants you. He sends accusing voices to surround you, not only to trouble you with outward battles but to assault your soul, causing you to lose hope. At the very moment it may look like you're surrounded by enemies, the Lord reveals Himself as an impenetrable shield surrounding your every side with glorious protection.

Here was David's testimony. "But you, O Lord, are a shield about me" (Psalm 3:3). An extraordinary truth is embedded in this verse. We're being told, in essence, "It may look like you're surrounded by enemies, but the truth is you are surrounded by God Himself. He is a shield protecting you on every side. No part of your life isn't covered by Him." David concluded the verse by calling God "my glory, and the lifter of my head."

This psalm begins with the prayer of a beleaguered king who despaired over the mounting odds stacked against him. By verse three, things begin to change. David had another prayer in his heart, a prayer of awesome hope. He had moved from being overwhelmed by "many, many, many" things to a single-minded focus on one thing: his source of deliverance. He was no longer worried about being surrounded by many trials but instead was lifted by the help he knew he had in God. Just when he was overwhelmed by the many enemies coming at him, David instead saw his shield, the Lord Himself, surrounding him against them all. Psalm 3 tells us that it doesn't matter how encircled we may be by oncoming trials. No matter what direction the assaults come from, the Lord has us covered. This is true for us not just in some circumstances but in all of them. God has control over all our concerns and worries and over all voices that may slander us. He is a shield that covers every inch of our being, leaving no opening for the enemy's piercing arrows.

The prophet Elisha testified to this truth. Second Kings describes a supernatural vision that God gave to Elisha and his young servant. The scene was a miraculous revelation—indeed, a manifestation—amid a terrible moment as the powerful Syrian army surrounded God's people completely. "When the servant of the man of God rose early in the morning and went out, behold, an army with horses and chariots was all around the city. And the servant said, 'Alas, my master! What shall we do?' He said, 'Do not be afraid, for those who are with us are more than those who are with them.' Then Elisha prayed and said, 'O LORD, please open his eyes that he may see.' So the Lord opened the eyes of the young man, and he saw, and behold, the mountain was full of horses and chariots of fire all around

Elisha" (2 Kings 6:15-17). These powerful images were a revelation of God's protective presence.

The word that David used for "shield" didn't signify an angelic host or some kind of supernatural force field. David literally meant what he said when he declared, "*You*, O LORD, are a shield about me" (Psalm 3:3, my emphasis). David knew his greatest shield was God's very presence. He was saying, "I know my safety and protection are not in my sword, nor in my horses or chariots, nor in a mighty army. Lord, I am shielded by your glorious presence. You alone are sufficient!" It doesn't matter what our problem is or even what our history with God is. If we have turned to Him, crying, "Jesus, my Savior and Lord," and are committed to following Him with our whole heart, then He shields and encompasses us fully.

In verse three, David identified three ways that God met him at his point of greatest need. First, the Lord was a shield to David; He was also David's glory. "But you, O Lord, are a shield about me, my glory, and the lifter of my head" (Psalm 3:3). The Hebrew word for "glory" here is *kavod*. It signifies a weightiness or great substance. God's presence isn't some light thing; it is deep and profound, real and long-lasting, not fleeting but instead leaving a mark.

Third, David testified that the Lord was the lifter of his head. God alone gives us the faith and confidence we need to face the long odds against us. When David was on the run, he reminded himself of Who God was, and that is when his confidence began to return. The Lord wants this for us, too. He shields us from the destruction our enemy seeks to bring upon us. The weighty substance of His glory clears away all self-doubt that keeps us mired in unworthiness, and His shed blood makes us worthy. Finally, God lifts our head, removing every hindrance to our belief in Him.

In the next verse, David made a loud, anguished cry of emotion. "I cried aloud to the Lord, and he answered me from his holy hill" (Psalm 3:4). In his moment of crisis, David made his pain known to God. This was no meek plea or lightly whispered request. David's cry was loud and anguished.

Many of us are afraid to be emotional before God. We fear if we let ourselves go, we might expose a character weakness or a lack of faith. We recoil at the thought of revealing all the doubts and fears we harbor inside. However, the Lord already knows the contents of our heart, and He wants us to express it all. Why? He wants our anguish removed from our heart and mind and transferred instead to His shoulders.

David knew this about the Lord, and that is why he cried out in prayer. He didn't reach out to his advisers for a plan or to his generals for a strategy or to his family for solace. He knew that God alone held the comfort he craved for his soul, the solution to his need, and the power to bring it all to pass.

Thus, David shifted his focus completely. He no longer dwelled on the increasing numbers of people who opposed him. Note the result of David's cry. "....and he answered me from his holy hill." This phrase contains three powerful words for every follower of Jesus: "He answered me." When we are surrounded, troubled, and weeping through our darkest night, Christ answers us. When we need hope of deliverance, we can know not only that He is there but that He will respond.

Be assured, David's loud cry wasn't merely a cathartic release of emotions. That would reduce God to a skillful psychologist who is limited to only making us feel better. No, He is Lord over all things including our trials and circumstances. In fact, He is always at work orchestrating a marvelous deliverance for us. Our cry initiates heaven's revelation to us that all our enemies are surrounded by God Himself. Elisha and his servant witnessed this reality firsthand.

How do we know that David received an answer? After all, there wasn't a single indication he would ever regain any of the precious things he lost. Absalom had not laid down his arms and was on an upward trajectory to power. No, David knew he had received an answer for one reason; he understood the heart of God. Before he even uttered his cry, David was on intimate terms with God's omniscience, omnipotence, and sovereignty. He knew that whatever the Lord chose for him was good.

God has a sovereign plan for all of us, and it cannot be thwarted. We are told in Scripture that before the foundation of the world, Christ's work of salvation was already on the move for us (see Ephesians 1:4). The bottom line is that we don't have to worry, fret or fear. We don't have to wonder whether our prayers are the right kind or whether we might expose something ugly about ourselves if we bare our souls before God. He hears our groaning both inward and outward, and He is orchestrating the events of our lives. In fact, when we bring our cries to Him, we align ourselves with the work His Spirit is already doing.

Verse four holds a key lesson: David worshiped before he prayed. In fact, his worship actually led to his intercession. Notice the sequence here: "O Lord, are a shield about me, my glory, and the lifter of my head. I cried aloud to the Lord" (Psalm 3:3-4). In verse three, David detailed the wonders of God's roles as his shield, glory, and lifter of his head. That praise led to his prayer in verse four. So you see, out of David's worship came a renewed confidence that he could be bold in prayer, knowing God would answer and move on his behalf. When we are in need, our first act doesn't have to be an urgent plea seeking a breakthrough. We benefit if we worship first, an action that reorients us to the source of our solutions.

Years ago, my father preached a memorable sermon called "Right Song, Wrong Side." It was about the song of worship the Israelites sang after God opened the Red Sea to deliver them from the pursuing Egyptians, whom He destroyed in the crashing waves. My father's message was that the Israelites would have had a stronger testimony if they had worshiped God while still in danger. In other words, we're not to wait until we've been delivered before we begin to worship the Lord. When David offered worship, he was at his lowest moment. That restored his confidence, and it made all the difference for him.

This kind of confidence puts fear into our attackers. They see that our power lies not in our circumstances or abilities but in God Himself. Don't wait for your circumstances to change before you begin to offer worship. Let the Lord change your heart through your worship, and you'll be completely reoriented for the battle you face.

David was able to sleep soundly despite every opposition facing him. "I lay down and slept" (Psalm 3:5). The context for this verse suggests that sleep came because God had lifted David's head, giving him peace. David had cast all his cares on the Lord and now he could rest. The next chapter says so explicitly. "In peace I will both lie down and sleep; for you alone, O Lord, make me dwell in safety" (Psalm 4:8).

The ability to sleep might not seem like that big of a deal. We grasp its significance, however, when our troubles mount and we spend nights tossing and turning with worry. Only then do we understand that sleep is sometimes a great answer to prayer. When we are blessed with sound sleep, our wellbeing is refreshed, renewed, and restored. "I woke again, for the LORD sustained me" (Psalm 3:5). With deep rest of soul, we have the mental vigor and physical vitality to reenter battle fueled by the Lord's sustaining strength.

Webster's Dictionary defines "sustain" as "to give support or relief to; to supply with sustenance, nourish; keep going, prolong." It may seem that with David's chaotic situation, God's promises weren't sustained at all. In fact, the opposite seemed true, that God's promises in David's life were completely disrupted. The truth is that those promises were maintained despite outward appearances. You see, David was still king according to the Lord's sovereignty, despite being ousted from the throne by a human enemy. The story bore out this truth; God soon restored David.

The same is true in our lives, no matter what our circumstances. He rules over all our steps at all times, a reality reflected not in appearances but on promises. David was telling us, "I woke to the realization that despite everything, God maintained His promise to me without interruption." This is good news for us when we are in the midst of trials. It's a promise that has power to sustain us.

First Samuel 17:1 tells us that at one point Absalom had 12,000 men who pursued David. Despite this, God's chosen king no longer feared. "I will not be afraid of many thousands of people who have set themselves against me all around" (Psalm 3:6). With his fear gone and his faith emboldened, David was stirred to petition God boldly for help. "Arise, O LORD! Save me, O my God!" (Psalm 3:7). David's heart was steady after that. His flight had turned into fight.

God gives us not only internal peace but external victories. It is one thing for us to reenter the battle saying, "I have peace to face this now." It is another for God to go before us into the battle and destroy our enemies. Deep down, we all want our outward circumstances to change. A Christian faith is not solely about internal victories but also about external victories. God can save marriages. He can set captives free from addictions. He can heal the sick and raise the dead. He can change our financial circumstances.

He can fill us with the Holy Spirit, transforming our hearts and renewing our minds. These are all external changes, whether physical, mental or material. Nothing is too difficult for God.

Moreover, God deals not just with some but all attacks against us. "For you strike all my enemies on the cheek; you break the teeth of the wicked" (Psalm 3:7). When God strikes, it is not with a light blow. His dealings are forceful, knocking out our enemies. It is revealing that "teeth" are mentioned in this verse. David's greatest pains came from the accusations of opponents, people who said there was no salvation for him in God. In this verse, David called on God to strike the physical source of those lies and shut them up. Like David, we know that God shuts the mouth of the great accuser, Satan.

"Salvation belongs to the LORD; your blessing be on your people!" (Psalm 3:8). This may sound like a kind of common, everyday benediction. It is much stronger than that. In fact, it may be the most important verse in Psalm 3. This verse declares that salvation belongs to Jesus; in other words, it is not our work. God is pleased with our faith, but faith comes through grace. Grace is the initiator, the result of Christ's finished work on the cross. "But to all who did receive him, who believed in his name, he gave the right to become children of God, who were born, not of blood nor of the will of the flesh nor of the will of man, but of God" (John 1:12-13). Salvation comes not by our doing but by God's.

David came to realize that all hope for the eternal establishment of his throne lay not in his own might or will but in the Spirit of the living God. This foreshadowed Christ's saving work on our behalf. It is all we need; we can put our hope, trust, and confidence in it.

When you began reading this chapter on Psalm 3, you may have felt like David when he fled his surrounding attackers. That was not the end of David's story, nor is your trial the end of your story. God is your hope in our time of trouble, a shield about you, the glory and the lifter of your head. He is faithful to see you through everything.

CHAPTER FOUR

Psalm 4
Demolishing Distress

To the choirmaster: with stringed instruments.
A Psalm of David.

1 Answer me when I call, O God of my righteousness!

　You have given me relief when I was in distress.

　Be gracious to me and hear my prayer!

2 O men,[a] how long shall my honor be turned into shame?

　How long will you love vain words and seek after lies? Selah

3 But know that the Lord has set apart the godly for himself;

　the Lord hears when I call to him.

4 Be angry, and do not sin;

　ponder in your own hearts on your beds, and be silent. Selah

5 Offer right sacrifices,

　and put your trust in the Lord.

6 There are many who say, "Who will show us some good?

　Lift up the light of your face upon us, O Lord!"

7 You have put more joy in my heart

　than they have when their grain and wine abound.

8 In peace I will both lie down and sleep;

　for you alone, O Lord, make me dwell in safety.

WE ALL KNOW WHAT IT'S like to be in distress, facing difficulties beyond our control. Psalm 4 tells us there is a cure for our distresses.

Most biblical scholars believe that this psalm is a continuation of the previous one. In Psalm 3, we saw David running for his life from his son Absalom. David found hope and solace in the midst of his crisis, yet here in Psalm 4 we see him crying out yet again. "Answer me when I call, O God of my righteousness! You have given me relief when I was in distress" (Psalm 4:1).

Throughout history, this psalm held a special significance for some Christian leaders. Thomas Brooks, one of my favorite Puritan authors, pointed out the importance of Psalm 4 to a great forefather in the faith, Chrysostom. "If he were the fittest in the world to preach a sermon to the whole world, and if he were to gather together one congregation and had some high mountain for his pulpit from whence he might have the prospect of the whole world in his view, and it were furnished him with a voice of brass, a voice as loud as the trumpets of the archangel, that all the world might hear him, he would choose to preach upon no other text than that in the Psalms, 'O mortal men, how long will ye love vanity, and follow after leasing [lies]?'" The verse that Brooks quoted here was Psalm 4:2.

Why did Thomas Brooks suppose that Chrysostom would choose to preach from this particular psalm? Of all the chapters in the Bible, why Psalm 4? Why not John 3 or Ephesians 5? The verse that Brooks quoted reflects why. It touches on the very nature of evil, the basic conflict we find ourselves struggling with in each generation. Psalm 4 also reflects an understanding of what it is like to be in distress and what the conflicts are that cause it. Every war has started because of a distress of some kind; every family conflict happens because of some distress. Psalm 4 shows us how to overcome the power that our distresses can have over us and

Ps. 4

instead to walk in faith, peace, and joy. It shows us a way of escape from the lies of vanity and material covetousness rather than succumbing to them. Most of all, it reveals the joy of our higher purpose through a life hid in Christ.

To back up a little bit, the first four psalms reveal a clear progression. Psalm 1 started with a primary, close-to-home kind of distress, that of personal temptation in the face of evildoers in our lives. Psalm 2 revealed the distress we experience when nations and peoples rage against God in the cosmic battle Satan wages against Christ and His church. Psalm 3 gave us a picture of internal distress whenever conflicts arise within the various realms of our lives, whether in family or church or community or beyond. The distresses of these categories can lead us to despondency or hopelessness. That brings us to Psalm 4, as David found himself still very much in the midst of an exterior battle that caused him internal distress.

When we last saw David, in Psalm 3, he had fled 12,000 soldiers who pursued him under orders from Absalom. Despite his terrible, agonizing distress, David testified that he was able to sleep soundly because the Lord gave him peace. Amazingly, he claimed he wasn't afraid of the thousands who hunted him and that he woke up with joy and fortitude. It is odd then to find in Psalm 4 that David was crying again, distressed by his circumstances. He opened the psalm by crying out, "Answer me when I call, O God of my righteousness!" (Psalm 4:1).

As we dive into this psalm, we see that it consists of three sections. The first section comprises what I call the intercession of distress. When we are in crisis, we become intercessors over our great need. The second section focuses on instruction for escaping distress. This involves not only praying and naming our request but also seeking the Lord's instruction to escape or navigate our crisis. The third and last part is about the impact when our distresses are demolished. This focus of this section is the effect on us, on others and on our world when we are delivered from distress.

The Hebrew word for "distress" has a much different meaning from that of the English word. In contemporary terms, whenever we speak of distress we usually mean tension or despair. The Hebrew word for distress reflects the idea of being in a tight or narrow space. It indicates a sense of being closed in, claustrophobic, confined on all sides. It might describe a military siege in which you're being bombarded day in and day out. You lack supplies to survive, and day by day your sense of peace drains away. The threat is so present and pressing that at some point you lose all hope of escaping. The apostle Paul used similar language when he wrote about his distresses. "We were pressed out of measure, above strength, insomuch that we despaired even of life" (2 Corinthians 1:8). The word for "distress" also suggests being crowded by opponents. What kind of opponents are causing your crisis and distress? These could be emotional, spiritual, physical, relational, financial, or something else.

Consider the reaction of God's people as they faced a crisis in 1 Samuel 13:6: "When the men of Israel saw that they were in trouble (for the people were hard pressed), the people hid themselves in caves and in holes and in rocks and in tombs and in cisterns." These Israelites' despair had to be awfully deep to send them fleeing to such crude hideaways.

David had that kind of distress as he fled Absalom. As he ran to survive, he cried out for God to end this horrible episode in his life. Maybe you've felt that kind of despair. Your crisis brought your spirit so low, emptying your heart of all hope, that the only thing you could do was run and hide. Each of us has been in that kind of state; if we haven't, we will. Isaiah famously wrote, "When the enemy shall come in like a flood . . ." (Isaiah 59:19, KJV). Note that he said "when" not "if." If you live long enough, you'll experience distressing opposition no matter how peacefully you try to live. Isaiah added, however, that when those enemies come, "the Spirit of the Lord shall lift up a standard against him" (Isaiah 59:19, KJV). The word "Spirit" in this verse can also mean "wind." In other words, in the midst of our crises, the Lord drives away our enemies the way the wind blows away dust.

When David made his cry in verse one, he had seen more distresses than many of us do in an entire lifetime. As a young shepherd, David had to fight for his life against bears, lions, and other wild beasts. As a soldier, he had to wage battles against mightier opponents. He had to evade the wrath of the king he served, a man so jealous he tried to kill David with a spear. Saul later sent soldiers to hunt down David, forcing him to live in caves. At one point, David's wife, Michal, had to rouse her husband from sleep as assassins approached. Imagine having to be let down from a window by your spouse to avoid being murdered. All of these urgent distresses pressed in on David and tightened around him.

I don't know about you, but after reading of David's distresses, I feel a lot better about my own. Everyone's distresses are legitimate, but David had more than his share. Moreover, he wasn't able to spend long periods seeking God for direction through his crises. At every turn, he needed escape routes to survive. Oftentimes, David's intercession was an urgent matter of getting instructions. At one point while on the run from Saul, David and his men saved the city of Keilah from the marauding Philistines. Afterward, David sought God for direction. The response he got was bluntly negative yet immensely helpful. "Then David said, 'O Lord, the God of Israel, your servant has surely heard that Saul seeks to come to Keilah, to destroy the city on my account. Will the men of Keilah surrender me into his hand? Will Saul come down, as your servant has heard? O LORD, the God of Israel, please tell your servant.' And the LORD said, 'He will come down.' Then David said, 'Will the men of Keilah surrender me and my men into the hand of Saul?' And the LORD said, 'They will surrender you'" (1 Samuel 23:10-12).

Anyone might despair to hear this news. David had just saved an entire city, yet if Saul were to show up, those same citizens he rescued would turn him in to an enemy. Talk about continually distressing circumstances; David couldn't get a break no matter where he turned. Our distresses may not be as continuously urgent as David's, but some are genuinely life-or-death. Many are "right now" situations, things that have to be resolved immediately. That's when intercession requires instruction.

Circumstantial distresses can lead to emotional ones. Almost always, our external distresses cause internal distress. We become fearful and anxious, tossing and turning at night, unable to sleep. That said, it is possible to have emotional peace in the midst of circumstantial distress. This can be true about not only our nights of turmoil but also our days of doing battle. We see this happening in Psalm 4, as David fled his pursuer, Absalom. When David cried to God in verse one, he hadn't lost the peace he obtained in Psalm 3; rather, I think he returned to the Lord to make sure his peace remained solid. If he couldn't control his distressing circumstances, he could at least have peace through the Holy Spirit.

In a later psalm, David spoke of the crises pressing in on him because of Saul's relentless pursuit. "My soul is in the midst of lions; I lie down amid fiery beasts—the children of man, whose teeth are spears and arrows, whose tongues are sharp swords" (Psalm 57:4). Reading this, we better understand David's opening cry, "Answer me when I call, O God of my righteousness! You have given me relief when I was in distress" (Psalm 4:1). We have studied the meaning of distress. Now let's look at the word "relief" in this verse, a condition David attributes to the Lord's intervention. The Hebrew word translated "relief" generally means to enlarge or grow wide. What does this mean in the context of distress? It means that God isn't just going to demolish our distress. He will also deliver us from a narrow, closed-in, hemmed-in place and cause us to grow and increase. In short, He'll replace our distress with blessing.

It is helpful for us to think of this enlarging in spiritual terms. The concept first appears in Exodus, when God spoke of the Promised Land. "For I will cast out nations before you and enlarge your borders" (Exodus 3:24). Note the two parts of this verse. In the first part, God said He would cast out Israel's enemies (demolishing their distress). In the second part, He said He would replace their distress with great blessing. They would no longer be confined, pressed in, and threatened but instead would be freed for blessings that increased. The prophet Isaiah used similar imagery when he wrote, "Enlarge the place of your tent, and let the curtains of your habitations be stretched out; do not hold back; lengthen your cords and strengthen your stakes" (Isaiah 54:2).

Isaiah's prophecy holds an amazing truth. No matter what happens in our life—even if it includes distresses like David's—we can be confident that God will see us through from crisis to blessing. He is trustworthy, faithful and good to us, and we can believe Him. David testified of this in Psalm 18, where he described at length the many distresses he and Israel had faced. "He brought me out into a broad place" (Psalm 18:19).

The themes we are talking about—being brought into a broad place to enlarge our tent—have been misused by certain movements within the church. For about a century now, various movements within the church have emphasized these verses. They make material increase the point of the Christian life. In short, the focus is a constant increase in blessings from job promotions to larger houses to nicer cars to immunity from sickness to personal influence to social prestige. There is nothing wrong with any of these things, but standing alone they comprise of a self-interest gospel. That is the opposite of Christ's Gospel.

God's purpose and calling on our lives is not to give us a larger footprint of material wealth and comfort in the world but to bring Jesus' awesome justice and all-surpassing comfort to others, and to do it in His name. The gospels make clear that Christ is after something in our souls; if we miss that, we will miss the mark completely. The biblical meaning behind the concept of increase is an enlarging of God's kingdom in our heart, to affect our household and our community. "I will run in the way of your commandments when you enlarge my heart" (Psalm 119:32). Christians and non-Christians alike can attain material wealth; only Christians can attain enlargement of faith, hope, peace, and joy. Oftentimes God accomplishes this paradoxically by revealing Himself through our distresses. He puts us in difficult straits, allowing us to be surrounded by enemies so that He may reveal His power on our behalf. Think about it! Our other-centered love often has its most powerful impact when we offer it generously despite our own lack.

A world in chaos needs a deep move of God. It needs a church that has been freed from all emotional bondage to distress. That kind of freedom is completely countercultural, confronting a worldly mindset. Psalm 4 addresses this. "O men, how long shall my honor be turned into shame? How long will you love vain words and seek after lies?" (Psalm 4:2). Our culture mocks and ridicules the righteous who live by the values of God's kingdom. As verse two shows, these worldly voices call the sacred profane and the profane sacred. In such a culture, one that shames the godly, God blesses the righteous in a way the world cannot know. How? He makes Himself known to His people. "But know that the LORD has set apart the godly for himself; the LORD hears when I call to him" (Psalm 4:3). In the short term, we may look defeated in the world's eyes; but in the long term, it is our opponents who will be shamed.

After David's heavy, devastating season, he re-ascended to the throne and was coronated once again. That is God's way in our lives, too. In verses two and three, David made clear, "You who taunt, scorn and suppress the truth know that God has His way and His people have their day." The phrase "set apart" in verse three reflects holiness. This in turn indicates the weightiness or substance that comes through life in Christ. In short, God uses our trials to develop in us a muscular spiritual strength. We can face any battle without cowering in fear or giving in to emotional distress because we know that through everything, we are more than conquerors in Christ. He does not abandon us in our crises; on the contrary, He is always present to us. Moreover, He actually identifies with us amid the world's scorn. "If the world hates you, know that it has hated me before it hated you. If you were of the world, the world would love you as its own; but because you are not of the world, but I chose you out of the world, therefore the world hates you" (John 15:18-19).

These are comforting words to those of us who feel distress because we stand out in a crowd. The King James Version actually calls us peculiar in the world's eyes, meaning special or set apart. "But ye are a chosen generation, a royal priesthood, an holy nation, a peculiar people; that ye should shew forth the praises of him who hath called you out of darkness into his marvellous light" (1 Peter 2:9, KJV). Two chapters later, Peter revealed the purpose of our peculiarity as well as the impact. "With respect to this they are surprised when you do not join them in the same flood of debauchery, and they malign you; but they will give account to him who is ready to judge the living and the dead. For this is why the gospel was preached even to those who are dead, that though judged in the flesh the way people are, they might live in the spirit the way God does" (1 Peter 4:4-6).

I encourage you never to compromise your stand for righteousness nor to lose your testimony as a countercultural Christian. Distresses will come from a mocking, slandering, cruel world; but you have been set apart by God Himself, whose purpose is revealed by the Spirit. We are given this comfort also: ". . . the LORD hears when I call to him" (Psalm 4:3).

I believe Psalm 4's instruction in our distress is twofold. The first part of Psalm 4's instruction is directed at our old man, meaning our unrighteous ways. The second part addresses our prophetic role as members of Christ's church. Verses four and five reveal this twofold instruction. "Be angry, and do not sin; ponder in your own hearts on your beds, and be silent. Offer right sacrifices, and put your trust in the Lord" (Psalm 4:4-5). We are told to be angry, and that begins with a hard look at our own sin. We are to grieve over our vain words and preoccupations ("How long will you love vain words and seek after lies?") and our pursuit of false gods ("Offer right sacrifices"). The Hebrew meaning of "be angry" suggests an agitation, meaning our sins should disturb us. We should be at the point of saying, "No more. I can't bear up under this kind of lifestyle. I've got to align my heart with the Lord's purposes for me."

The second way to be angry is at the culture of the current generation. Lot and Noah were examples of this, each grieving over the wickedness of their generation. Many of us today, however, are uncomfortable at merely having anger even when it is holy. Often in the church we're discouraged from being angry. We restrain or subdue that impulse rather than expressing it. According to the psalmist, however, being angry is a calling of God. We not only have the right to be angry but are obligated to be.

Angry at what, you ask? Angry at the global antichrist spirit, at the condition of the world, at the condition of our nation and at the church's spiritual decline. All of these things call for a holy anger to give voice to righteousness. God puts that in our heart. To be less than angry at such things may reflect an uncaring heart, one lacking concern or passion. That said, we are to "be angry, and do not sin." This command contains both a calling and a caution. In other words, it matters how we carry out our anger. We don't respond to the world with slander, ridicule, or mockery; that would be doing battle with the world on its terms. The Bible makes clear that we don't fight with man-made weapons, that ours are spiritual for pulling down strongholds (and, in this case, demolishing distresses). The Holy Spirit empowers us to have anger without sinning. In this way, we're able to fight our battles with a right spirit so that when we lie down to sleep, we do so in total peace. "Ponder in your own hearts on your beds, and be silent" (Psalm 4:4).

Instruction continues in the next verse. "Offer right sacrifices, and put your trust in the Lord" (Psalm 4:5). It is important to acknowledge our emotional distresses. This verse shows us how. First, we align our hearts properly before Him, and then we cast all our cares upon Him. Finally, the third part of Psalm 4 speaks of impact. As the Lord demolishes our distresses, we see the impact in our lives and in the world around us. The final three verses of Psalm 4 speak to this. "There are many who say, 'Who will show us some good? Lift up the light of your face upon us, O Lord!' You have put more joy in my heart than they have when their grain and wine abound. In peace I will both lie down and sleep; for you alone, O Lord, make me dwell in safety" (Psalm 4:6-8).

The same people who shame and ridicule Christians also lament, "Is there any good at all in this world?" They may have thought their wealth would contain all the good they sought. They may have thought that having political power would achieve the good they seek. They may have thought their worldly successes would supply the answers for which their souls hunger. Instead, they conclude, "Something is missing." In a darkened world, even the most cynical nonbelievers clamor for meaning.

David testified of the Lord, "You have put more joy in my heart than they have when their grain and wine abound" (Psalm 4:7). "Grain and wine" here suggest both food that is plenteous and drink that is festive. David was saying that he had more treasure in the Lord than all the wealth these partiers could ever own. They put their hope in their great abundance and yet hunger for something more real. Despite their unbelief, they long to see that something glorious exists. We are called to show them that glorious good, that indeed something amazing exists that is different from anything the world has to offer. The psalmist proclaims that one lowly, set-apart person whom the Lord hears possesses more than all the wealth in the world. When onlookers ask, "What good is in the world?," that godly person can answer, "I can show you good. It lies in the power of God. He is the way out of hellish despair."

The impact of having our distresses demolished is personal for us too. It manifests in a countenance of joy. A person of abundance can lack a truly, deeply rooted joy, but for the set-apart person, joy is a continual reality. Isaiah described this in an interesting passage about a man's dreams. "As when a hungry man dreams, and behold, he is eating, and awakes with his hunger not satisfied, or as when a thirsty man dreams, and behold, he is drinking, and awakes faint, with his thirst not quenched, so shall the multitude of all the nations be that fight against Mount Zion" (Isaiah 29:8). This man dreams that he eats and drinks his fill, but he wakes up empty. What is missing for him? He lacks the substance and weightiness that God's presence provides to all who call on Him. According to Isaiah, a life without God is only a dream compared to the substantive reality found in the Lord.

As the people of God, we are fulfilled in heart while not distressed over what we may lack. Our circumstances may be distressing, but that distress will be demolished. "Though the fig tree should not blossom, nor fruit be on the vines, the produce of the olive fail and the fields yield no food, the flock be cut off from the fold and there be no herd in the stalls, yet I will rejoice in the Lord; I will take joy in the God of my salvation. God, the Lord, is my strength; he makes my feet like the deer's; he makes me tread on my high places" (Habakkuk 3:17-19).

Thus, the psalmist is able to say in the final verse, "In peace I will both lie down and sleep; for you alone, O LORD, make me dwell in safety" (Psalm 4:8). In this world, it is easy to be overcome by anxiety and fear. Not so for those who belong to the Lord. The last verse of Psalm 4 is a promise of peace. When your life isn't about amassing an abundance of grain and wine, you don't fear losing any of that. Instead, you can cry out as David did, "Answer me when I call, O God of my righteousness!," and you can conclude alongside him, "You alone, O Lord, make me dwell in safety." A hungry, waiting world will see the difference.

CHAPTER FIVE

Psalm 5
Watch What God Will Do

1 Give ear to my words, O Lord;

consider my groaning.

2 Give attention to the sound of my cry,

my King and my God,

for to you do I pray.

3 O Lord, in the morning you hear my voice;

in the morning I prepare a sacrifice for you and watch.

4 For you are not a God who delights in wickedness;

evil may not dwell with you.

5 The boastful shall not stand before your eyes;

you hate all evildoers.

6 You destroy those who speak lies;

the Lord abhors the bloodthirsty and deceitful man.

7 But I, through the abundance of your steadfast love,

will enter your house.

I will bow down toward your holy temple

in the fear of you.

8 Lead me, O Lord, in your righteousness

because of my enemies;

make your way straight before me.

9 For there is no truth in their mouth;

their inmost self is destruction;

their throat is an open grave;

they flatter with their tongue.

10 Make them bear their guilt, O God;

let them fall by their own counsels;

because of the abundance of their transgressions cast them out,

for they have rebelled against you.

11 But let all who take refuge in you rejoice;

let them ever sing for joy,

and spread your protection over them,

that those who love your name may exult in you.

12 For you bless the righteous, O Lord;

you cover him with favor as with a shield.

THE TITLE OF THIS CHAPTER comes from verse three of this psalm. ". . . in the morning I prepare a sacrifice for you and watch" (Psalm 5:3). The psalmist here was David, and he wrote this while still in trouble, evading and battling enemies and grieving his losses. On the surface, and without any clarifying context, this verse can sound as if David kept watch in order to stay on guard and protect himself. Instead, David was watching for what God would do. The verse that follows tells us why. "For you are not a God who delights in wickedness; evil may not dwell with you" (Psalm 5:4). David was surrounded by wickedness; and because he knew God's character, he realized the Lord would not allow that evil to continue.

Psalm 5 shows David writing about the same struggles as in the psalms that precede it. He endured a personal attack on his family from within his own family. He struggled over the difficulties going on in his nation. He had hoped he would be relieved of all these situations by the time he composed this psalm, but they continued day after day.

David's heart had to be weary. He had a persistent inner pain due to his unrelenting problems. His enemies still surrounded him. His son Absalom, who had driven David from the throne, had not gone away. In the preceding psalms, David had sung songs of hope and trust in the Lord, but his circumstances clearly had not changed. *his strength came*

If I were David, I would have struggled with uncertainty. Did David *from staying in God's* ever wonder, "Is God hearing my prayers?" In this psalm, he didn't start off *presence* as he usually did, recounting past works of God and worshiping Him with thanksgiving. That is an example to all of us; we ought to seek the Lord in worshipful gratitude for His awesome faithfulness. David bypassed that in Psalm 5, not because he was remiss but, ironically, because of his humility. He was unashamed of his bare need, and he opened the psalm by expressing that need. "Give ear to my words, O LORD; consider my groaning" (Psalm 5:1). David was saying, "Lord, I have aching wounds in my heart, and all I can bring to you is my groaning. I am in crisis mode, so I'm coming to you straight away with my naked need."

The Lord does not despise this kind of prayer. Note the opening word, "Give." Some of us would be self-conscious to make that our first word of prayer to God. "Lord, give me . . . " Yet that is exactly how Jesus taught us to pray and to do it regularly and unashamedly. "Give us this day our daily bread" (Matthew 6:11). God desires that we come to Him with every need, acknowledging Him as the giver of all good things. It is no shame to pray, "Lord, please, open that door, solve this problem, fix my crisis. Would You somehow give me hope amid the surrounding storm?"

David began Psalm 5 with a direct, vibrant, passionate plea to the Lord for help, and he had no doubt God would faithfully meet his need. Like many other psalms, this one can be broken into several sections. These sections represent David's four stages as he moved through his situation. He recognized, reset, realized, and rejoiced.

Our first action in an overwhelming crisis is to do as David did—to recognize the situation around us. The first thing we see in any trial is our pressing circumstance. The act of recognition, however, calls us to see something additional: the weariness in our spirit caused by our situation. We may feel needy and helpless, and we have to acknowledge this. David opens Psalm 5 with a cry to the Lord of naked honesty of heart. It shows us we can come to God with no sense of hindrance, knowing He has an answer for us in our utter need.

We also have to recognize that what we're asking for isn't a human resource; it comes from the heavenly Father. David was the leader of his nation, both politically and militarily, yet he didn't ask God for armor or for diplomatic wisdom or to rally other nations to his side. No, in his anxiety, stress, and weariness, David sought the heart of God for what God wanted for him. He trusted the Lord as the faithful, omniscient Giver of all good things, most especially in his times of urgent need.

This was a powerful shift for David in his state, and we are wise to pay attention to it. He was saying, "Lord, You not only know what I need most, but You also direct all the circumstances of my life. Only Your sovereign will can change it all." In essence, David was asking the Lord to move things not in the direction of his own heart's desires but in the direction of God's heart. That is significant.

In fact, David's request of the Lord—"Give ear" or "Listen"—aligns with the sovereignty embedded in the Lord's Prayer. You see, the Lord's Prayer is both a petition and an acknowledgment. Behind the request for daily sustenance—"Give us this day our daily bread"—is a faith that acknowledges, "God, everything comes from Your hand, and I believe You have all things under control." David's faith allowed him to have joy as he composed the rest of Psalm 5. In the midst of his pressing circumstances, he understood, "Lord, You are sovereign, and I can trust You."

The second thing we're to do in crisis is to reset. The concept of resetting appears in verse three. "O Lord, in the morning you hear my voice; in the morning I prepare a sacrifice for you and watch" (Psalm 5:3). David was saying, "Lord, I am waiting and watching. I've got my eyes open to whatever You're going to do next." David opened this psalm in a desperate state of distress. Two verses later, he was resetting his thought patterns and emotions. He knew that God heard his prayers, and thus he could give thanks, willing to wait in faith for God to act. In short, David realigned himself with God's trustworthiness and faithfulness. This was quite a turnaround. I can only imagine the many nights David wasn't able to sleep, tossing and turning, nodding off then waking in a panic. At times in my life, I could relate to that. When things are falling apart, our imaginations can run wild with the many terrible outcomes that could happen.

David remedied that for himself by resetting his heart and mind. He woke in the morning with praise to the Lord, determined to set his thoughts on the things of God. He would pray, in essence, "My life is not my own but yours, O Lord." Again, this aligns with the Lord's Prayer: "Your kingdom come, your will be done, on earth as it is in heaven" (Matthew 6:10). Part of resetting is preparing to watch what God will do. We serve a sovereign God of miracles, and we can say of Him with confidence, "Nothing is too difficult for the Lord." When we practice the spiritual discipline of resetting, we find the courage, hope, and trust that has been missing from our lives. Before, all we could do was watch and worry; now, in faith, we watch to see God act.

After this, David made another shift. He turned his focus back to the wicked. "For you are not a God who delights in wickedness; evil may not dwell with you. The boastful shall not stand before your eyes; you hate all evildoers. You destroy those who speak lies; the Lord abhors the bloodthirsty and deceitful man" (Psalm 5:4-6). This may seem as if David was ping-ponging back and forth between deep trust in the Lord and great worry over his enemies. Many of us do this when we're under intense stress. Note, however, the way that David framed his shift of focus. On the one hand, he acknowledged, "Lord, all these evildoers stand before You boasting. They're bloodthirsty and deceitful, and they're still present in my life, surrounding me with evil plans." At the same time, David saw these threatening enemies as under the sovereign hand of a God Who would not tolerate their evildoing: "The Lord abhors the bloodthirsty and deceitful man." Here was yet another reset by David. The sovereignty of God allowed him to see his own weariness and to know the Lord would act against his enemies. So while David was at his lowest point, with no strength of heart or mind, his faith stirred him to wait and watch in faith.

The third thing we do in crisis mode is to realize the demise of evildoers. We have to realize that God's enemies will be brought low by His mighty arm. Who are His enemies? They're people of a depraved mind who denounce what is good in the world, calling it evil and calling evil good. They mock those who try to do good, including those who follow Jesus. In verse four, David wrote that God's enemies will not be able to continue in their ways. "For you are not a God who delights in wickedness; evil may not dwell with you" (Psalm 5:4).

 God cannot abide evil. Therefore, we can know that the enemies surrounding us will be brought down and the problems they cause will be destroyed. "You destroy those who speak lies" (Psalm 5:6). The wicked may have their moment, but David showed us what it means to wait in faith and watch what God will do.

This brings us to a verse that some Christians don't know what to do with. " . . . you hate all evildoers" (Psalm 5:5). Maybe you've wondered as some believers do, "Does God really hate? How is that possible?" Most of us are uncomfortable with the idea of our loving God hating something, yet David's statement that God hates all evildoers isn't problematic; it is both profound and instructive.

A popular phrase is used freely in the church today: "God hates the sin but loves the sinner." We all get the gist of this, but in a sense this phrase separates the sinner from the sin in a way that bypasses the sin committed. Scripture makes clear that God has something different in mind.

In Malachi's prophecy, the Lord connected the sinner with the sin and with righteous judgment. "Esau I have hated. I have laid waste his hill country and left his heritage to jackals of the desert" (Malachi 1:3). In the New Testament, Paul connected willful evildoers with the Lord's destruction. "And since they did not see fit to acknowledge God, God gave them up to a debased mind to do what ought not to be done. They were filled with all manner of unrighteousness, evil, covetousness, malice. They are full of envy, murder, strife, deceit, maliciousness. They are gossips, slanderers, haters of God, insolent, haughty, boastful, inventors of evil, disobedient to parents, foolish, faithless, heartless, ruthless. Though they know God's righteous decree that those who practice such things deserve to die, they not only do them but give approval to those who practice them" (Romans 1:28-32). Paul said of such evildoers, "the wrath of God is revealed from heaven against all ungodliness and unrighteousness of men" (Romans 1:18).

We know that God so loves the world that He gave His begotten Son for it, and this love includes all sinners. His sovereign desire is that all humankind would repent and be saved. On one hand, Scripture gives us a powerful sense of God's love, yet we cannot deny the equally powerful sense in Scripture of what God hates. He can love the world and the people in it and yet also hate what those people do, hate the wickedness they bring, and hate the harm and destruction they cause in others' lives. This twofold character of loving and hating does not end with God. It has to be part of our lives, transforming our hearts, and informing our minds. If we have God's love in us, we're going to hate the evil done by those who oppose His love. For instance, if you love children, you're going to hate abortion and child abuse. If you love peace, you're going to hate war and the death and destruction it brings. God is love, and He is also just, which means He hates evil. In His awesome, just love, He won't stand by forever while evil is done. In time, He will pour out His wrath of righteous justice upon wicked evildoers.

"You destroy those who speak lies; the LORD abhors the bloodthirsty and deceitful man" (Psalm 5:6). This speaks of people who are out for violence, looking to render great pain. The Lord abhors their actions, lies, deceit, and bloodthirstiness; and He brings destruction down on all who practice them. Three verses later, David took up this theme again. "For there is no truth in their mouth; their inmost self is destruction; their throat is an open grave; they flatter with their tongue. Make them bear their guilt, O God; let them fall by their own counsels" (Psalm 5:9-10). This is strong language. We don't hear this kind of expression very often in the church. As Christians, we lean toward a softer culture, not saying such things publicly or out loud for fear of coming across as severe. For David, however, these were expressions of theological truth, and he delivered them very publicly. The context for him was not personal vengeance; rather, it was "Watch what God will do to destroy evil."

So how do we interpret this psalm in terms of our own trials? I don't believe God will necessarily cast people out from our lives when they oppose us; there will always be people who oppose us. Instead, He might desire to see our situation resolved in a relational way. Jesus addressed this again and again in the gospels. Though our troublers are fellow humans, the Lord may use our conflict with them to address an issue of our heart. For example, He may want to cast out a certain fear or a quick temper rather than a person. In any case, He is faithfully at work, and David told us the Lord won't let evildoers continue in their ways. God is sovereign over them, too, controlling what they can and can't do. He will ultimately stop their wicked plots.

This is a recurring theme throughout Psalms. In fact, it will come up again soon, in the chapter on Psalm 7. There we read, "Behold, the wicked man conceives evil and is pregnant with mischief and gives birth to lies. He makes a pit, digging it out, and falls into the hole that he has made. His mischief returns upon his own head, and on his own skull his violence descends" (Psalm 7:14-16). In writing these passages, David was realizing the demise of evildoers. They may dig pits for us to fall into, he said, but they will be the ones who fall into them. Meanwhile, God will raise us up, protect us and lead us through out trials. Workers of wickedness won't have the final say. In placing our confidence in the Lord's sovereignty, we find power to be patient, to wait and to endure as God works to end the evil plots against us.

The fourth thing we're to do in crisis mode is rejoice in the protective refuge that God provides us. David continued, "I, through the abundance of your steadfast love, will enter your house" (Psalm 5:7). The phrase "enter your house" refers to being in God's presence. Be definition, our enemies will be shut off from us because they can't dwell near the Lord's presence.

They may rant and rave, but they can't enter the place of peace where God protects us. From within that safe dwelling, we'll watch God move in amazing sovereignty. How does such a refuge come about for us? David described: " . . . through the abundance of your steadfast love." Here was yet another kind of reset for David. He reentered an understanding of God's love. This leads to David's plea in the next verse. "Lead me, O Lord, in your righteousness because of my enemies; make your way straight before me" (Psalm 5:8). David was admitting, "Lord, my enemies can derail me. My life is totally vulnerable right now, and those who oppose me can throw me off and send me into doubt and fear. Lead me back into a right understanding of Your faithful love. Then my enemies won't be able to derail me from the things You have for me."

David rejoiced over being led in the straight way. He knew God's way was different from his own. Left to his own wits, he might have tried planning an escape from his trials. He may have prayed, "God, here is what I want to happen to my enemies. Here is the closure I want for my problems." Instead, David stated, "My confidence is in a sovereign God. I'm going to trust You, O Lord, to make the way straight before me." David then preached this revelation to everyone. "But let all who take refuge in you rejoice; let them ever sing for joy, and spread your protection over them, that those who love your name may exult in you" (Psalm 5:11). Like David, we are able to rejoice because God has provided us a refuge. No enemy can break through the protection that God puts around us. No matter how intense our trials become, we are shielded by God's sovereignty. According to David, we exult in the Lord as we see all He is doing.

With that thought, David ended the psalm. "For you bless the righteous, O Lord; you cover him with favor as with a shield" (Psalm 5:12). What a statement. We are blessed by God to the point that we are covered with

His favor. It is easy to misread this verse because the concept of favor is so misconstrued and thus misunderstood. We've been led to think of favor as being showered with material goods, prospering in terms of possessions, fame or advancement. So how could someone like David—a man clearly in a fallen, sinful state—be favored by God? The key to this question rests in one powerful word anchoring this verse: "righteous." David believed God sovereignly made him righteous, and therefore he was in the right, as opposed to his enemies, who were unjust. He had committed injustices, but by turning from it and pursuing justice, God's grace made him righteous.

This final verse in Psalm 5 isn't just a nice benediction. For David, the closing verse of Psalm 5 was an essential reality, and it is for us, too. It involves real-life protection from our enemies and the ultimate destruction of all evil. Even if our enemies aren't destroyed, or our circumstances don't change, or the events of our lives don't work out the way we want, we are still able to rejoice in the refuge God has given us. We have favor through His shed blood for us, which cleanses and sanctifies us. We are renewed in spirit by being reconciled to Him. We are renewed in mind by having right thoughts about the Lord. Finally, we are renewed in hope by the promise of eternal life. Our refuge is not only protection from our enemies but the promise of being in the Lord's presence forever. By the end of Psalm 5, David's eyes were no longer focused on the temporal things of the world but instead were fixed on an eternal God. May the same be true of our spiritual vision.

Dark days may come to our nation and culture, with things beyond our control. Amid it all, Scripture tells us to look upward because our redemption draws near. I thank God for David's message from his own dark days that the Lord makes His people righteous in heart, mind, and spirit. In all things, our hope is in the Lord. Don't shrink back from praying,

"God, give me . . ." Then stand firm and watch what the Lord will do. Thank Him ahead of time for defeating your enemies, destroying your difficult circumstances, and bringing you into a place of safety and security.

David still had not recovered his throne, yet his faith in the Lord was rekindled. Remember for yourself the four R's that this psalm gives us all. Recognize your weariness in the battle. Reset your eyes on Christ. Realize the demise of every enemy that comes against you. Finally, rejoice in the all-protective, omnipotent refuge you have in the Lord. You have been blessed with the favor of God.

CHAPTER SIX

Psalm 6

The Goodness of God in Deferring Deliverance

1 O Lord, rebuke me not in your anger,

nor discipline me in your wrath.

2 Be gracious to me, O Lord, for I am languishing;

heal me, O Lord, for my bones are troubled.

3 My soul also is greatly troubled.

But you, O Lord—how long?

4 Turn, O Lord, deliver my life;

save me for the sake of your steadfast love.

5 For in death there is no remembrance of you;

in Sheol who will give you praise?

6 I am weary with my moaning;

every night I flood my bed with tears;

I drench my couch with my weeping.

7 My eye wastes away because of grief;

it grows weak because of all my foes.

8 Depart from me, all you workers of evil,

for the Lord has heard the sound of my weeping.

9 The Lord has heard my plea;

the Lord accepts my prayer.

10 All my enemies shall be ashamed and greatly troubled;
they shall turn back and be put to shame in a moment.

PSALM 6 IS A RECORD of David's cry to the Lord from a place of unfathomable pain. This psalm is remarkable for containing in one brief writing almost all the pain, sorrow, trials, and tribulations a human being can go through. Rarely do we find in one concise expression the struggles that come to us in every area of life, arenas central to our existence but that are overcome with problems. In these ten short verses, David described being confronted with the most prevailing and prominent forms of suffering possible.

When David wrote Psalm 6, he faced painful issues of body, soul, sin, enemies, and mortality. This is essentially all of human suffering in a nutshell. David experienced both physical sickness and anguish of soul. He spoke of Sheol and the fear of death. He referenced Satan and workers of evil who came against him.

To struggle with the pain and sorrow that comes with sin, to deal with debilitating health problems, to be attacked by enemies without cause and to be brought low in soul to the point of fearing death— We're all familiar with these kinds of trials to varying degrees. David faced all these things at once, and Psalm 6 is his desperate outcry to God. Also in this psalm, though, there is great hope for deliverance, healing, forgiveness and reconciliation with God. It is a picture of David seeking mercy as he faced the Lord's wrath and anger over his sins. We see him longing to prevail over realms of darkness brought on by those sins. He envisioned his enemies being eliminated from his life. He foresaw victory and conquest over all the things affecting him. His psalm is a vision of hope for each of us in all of our trials.

One cry from David encompassed all of his sufferings: "O Lord— how long?" (Psalm 6:3). As David listed all of his agonies, embedded in the midst of them was a question: "How long?" "How long will this continue, God? How long do I have to suffer until You hear my cry? How long do I have to endure this excruciating pain in my body? I am physically wasting away." (When David wrote verse three, "O Lord, for my bones are troubled," the Hebrew suggests a deadly disease.) "How long will I be downcast in my soul? I'm troubled, worried, fearful, and discouraged. How long will my soul be chained in anguish? When will You free me, encourage my heart, lift me up and let me taste victory again?"

I believe that at various times in our lives, we all share David's fear of death. He pleaded with God not to let him die. "For in death there is no remembrance of you; in Sheol who will give you praise?" (Psalm 6:5). David spoke for many of us. God has given us great and precious promises, yet why must we endure long seasons when His promises seem nowhere to be found? I have cried out like David did over my own anguished trials. "Lord, how long until I experience Your promise of abundant life? How long will I have sleepless nights over my prodigal son? How long until my back injury is healed? Will this threat of cancer last my whole life? The circumstances You've allowed me to face have formed a perpetual cloud over me. It hangs above my thoughts day after day, month after month, year after year. How many nights will I go sleepless over all the things I'm facing?"

In some circles, cries like these are called existential dread. We wake in the morning, thinking, "Something is wrong, but I don't know what it is. I can't put my finger on it, yet it affects every area of my life. I never feel God's victory anymore. Instead, I'm plagued by this vague dread I can't describe. O Lord, where are Your promises in my life? Why have they disappeared?" David captured this in three verses. "Be gracious to me, O Lord, for I am languishing; heal me, O Lord, for my bones are troubled. My soul also is greatly troubled. But you, O Lord—how long?" (Psalm 6:2-3).

God's goodness is revealed in deferring our deliverance. With a mere snap of His finger, a wink of His eye, or a breath from His nostrils, God could resolve every one of our trials and sufferings. So is the Lord instead working a greater purpose in our life than what could be accomplished through an instantaneous deliverance? Is He creating from our troubles something better that is for our good? In short, is there some discipleship behind His discipline?

The apostle Paul wrote, "Though our outer self is wasting away, our inner self is being renewed day by day. For this light momentary affliction is preparing for us an eternal weight of glory beyond all comparison, as we look not to the things that are seen but to the things that are unseen. For the things that are seen are transient, but the things that are unseen are eternal" (2 Corinthians 4:16-18). Our trials and tribulations are transient and fleeting compared to eternity. However, as we endure them, they can work a greater, more powerful victory in our lives than is evident to us in our suffering. This happens for God's eternal purposes and is all within His great, encompassing love for us.

We know from the end of David's story that God was doing just that. He was deferring deliverance for His servant with something greater in mind not only for the king but for the nation of Israel. Thus, those words "How long?" are meant to be instructive to us. They are a cry of continued longing. You see, for as long as we cry these two words, a great work is taking place in our hearts. "How long?" is a cry of faith; it is uttered from a deep knowledge that God does indeed deliver. From Genesis to Revelation, God's Word makes it clear that when people find themselves in a terrible situation, they can turn to Him and He will deliver them faithfully.

The truth is that God's deferring of our deliverance is where the rubber meets the road in terms of our faith. Sometimes our periods of waiting cause our souls more anguish than even our trial. We know God is good, but how can we know His goodness when we're in constant suffering? As David wrote, "For in death there is no remembrance of you; in Sheol who will give you praise?" (Psalm 6:5). Is there truly goodness in God's deferring of our deliverance? Yes, God is good when He defers our deliverance. One of our mistakes in thinking about this is that we see deliverance as solely circumstantial. In reality, some troubles simply won't be resolved on this side of heaven.

You may have heard of Charles Spurgeon, the great English minister of the nineteenth century. His anointed preaching led countless thousands to the Lord. As great as this man's gifts were for the kingdom of God, Spurgeon still struggled with a lifelong depression. From what we know about depression today, it is likely that Spurgeon's trial was more than an emotional condition; its roots were probably mental and physical as well. He never was freed from depression during his days on earth, yet we know that in Heaven this humble servant of God knows ultimate healing.

Our ongoing struggles with sin are an example of God's deferred deliverance. We may know healing and deliverance from sin, yet we are not fully free from its pull. We are told throughout Scripture to be on guard against it. The same is true of having enemies in life. People may oppose us for their own reasons or for no reason, and for most of us, that will be a lifelong reality. Deliverance from some things is simply going to be deferred until we get to heaven. If we don't face these realities, we risk harboring anger at God for life's disappointments. This has the potential to derail our faith. We can end up pointing our finger at God and saying, "You broke Your promise! You didn't deliver me when I prayed for release. How can I ever trust Your word?"

Every promise of God is true; He never lies. If His promises are delayed, it is not because He's incapable of delivering us; but rather, it's meant for His greater purposes. He is working some greater good in our life, soul, heart, mind, and relationship with Him. We can be sure that an amazing, eternal work is being accomplished from within our every cry. Therefore, it is never futile to cry out over any of our trials. "How long, O Lord, will I be sick and go unhealed? How long will my soul be downcast, bereft of all encouragement? How long will thoughts of death cause me to wake up with dread? How long will I endure attacks from enemies? How long will I be tempted to sin, seeking some kind of relief from my unrelenting troubles? How long, O Lord, until You break apart these trials and free me? How long until I know joy again?"

Of all the "how long" questions David asks, the first one he cried out was over his sin. Five times in this psalm David asked the question, "How long?" The first "how long" had to do with his sin. David opened the psalm pleading, "O Lord, rebuke me not in your anger, nor discipline me in your wrath" (Psalm 6:1). He struggled with sin, as did his predecessor, Saul. On first glance, David's sins looked at lot worse than Saul's, seeming much more serious by comparison. For example, the first time Saul was publicly called out for his sin was over a sacrifice he made before battle. The prophet Samuel had told Saul to wait for him before making the sacrifice, but Samuel was delayed in arriving. Impatient to enter battle, Saul hurried the sacrifice, and God was displeased. Maybe worse than this was that Saul, having lost the kingdom, consulted a witch who called up a spirit from the dead. Certainly, God hated that. Saul lost and never recovered his vital connection with the Lord.

Now take David's sins and weigh them against Saul's. David lusted after a married woman, Bathsheba, and sent for her to come to his palace. There, David committed adultery with her and got her pregnant. Bathsheba happened to be married to one of David's top military leaders, Uriah. To cover up his sins, David called Uriah back from the front lines, hoping the soldier would sleep with Bathsheba and thus think the baby was his own; but Uriah declined that luxury while his men were dying at war. When David's plan failed, he complicated his sin by doing the unthinkable: He set up Uriah, his own loyal soldier, to die in battle. It was premeditated murder, and the plan worked. David tried to hide it, but the prophet Nathan knew what happened and called out David on his awful sins.

As I read about David's anguish of soul in this psalm, I can't help thinking that he was reviewing his awful sins. He imagined the judgment he deserved and feared it would be like Saul's. "The Lord is rightfully angry with me. I have earned His wrath. Will His discipline be the same for me that He meted out to Saul? Will He take the kingdom from me? If it happens, I would deserve it. I am not worthy of the Lord's love." How many times have you had similar thoughts when things began falling apart in your life? "I'm not a worthy vessel. My sins have disqualified me. I'm not good enough to call myself a Christian." My response to you is that David and Saul weren't worthy vessels either. None of us comes to the Lord in worthiness, yet He accepts us.

So why was David ultimately forgiven when Saul was ultimately rejected? I believe the difference was in their repentance. Saul's repentance was self-centered, not focused on the Lord. He was preoccupied with his own dishonor rather than God's honor. David's repentance was the opposite, completely God-centric. He wrote, "For I know my transgressions, and my sin is ever before me. Against you, you only, have I sinned and done what is evil in your sight, so that you may be justified in your words and blameless in your judgment" (Psalm 51:3-4). Of course, David's sin wasn't solely against God as he said here. His sins against others were grievous, bringing shame on his household through his adultery, recklessly impregnating a married woman, and taking the life of a soldier who trusted him as a military leader. The difference was that David was utterly broken over what he'd done. He was especially concerned with his relationship to the Lord, which was his reason for living. This sickness of soul may have been the reason for David's brokenness of health and of body. I picture all of this haunting him as he was driven from the throne in Jerusalem. I would not be surprised if David wondered, "How long will my sins rule over me? I can't expect anything but the Lord's wrath and death." David's sin created a fear in his heart, dreading God's anger and judgment.

David believed in the wrath of God, but a lot of Christians today have an aversion to this doctrine. A denomination recently sought to change the words of a hymn that speaks of God's wrath being satisfied at the cross. They want to replace the words "wrath" and "satisfied" with softer terms. Their aim was to make a "safe zone" for Christians who don't want to face the depth of their sin and God's righteous justice. As David knew, however, the Lord is a God of judgment who does get angry and whose wrath is stirred by evil. We can't look at Scripture honestly and come away with anything other than those realities.

Even so, there are voices in the church that also take offense to the idea that a just God would punish His innocent Son on behalf of the guilty. They ask, "Who but a tyrant would kill His own innocent son?"

They call this doctrine divine child abuse. What they are condemning, exactly, is the Christian doctrine of substitutionary atonement. In simple terms, this is the belief that Christ died in our place, taking the world's sins upon Himself and bearing the wrath that is stirred in God by those sins. Right now, substitutionary atonement is one of the most despised, rejected, and ignored doctrines in many pulpits. Critics ask, "Why the need for blood? Why does God demand sacrifice? Why can't He be good and forgiving as is His nature?" The condemnation of this doctrine misses something crucial to the Christian faith. What it lacks is a grasp of the depth of human depravity, the evil it creates and how much God hates it. It also lacks an understanding of the holiness, beauty, and majesty of God, all of which are manifest in His creation. These things—God's transformative goodness and humankind's abject sin—stand in stark contrast, clear for all the world to see.

Think of all the passages in Scripture stating that darkness can't coexist with light nor evil with good. Jesus said so. "A healthy tree cannot bear bad fruit, nor can a diseased tree bear good fruit" (Matthew 7:18). Paul took up this subject in his epistle to the Romans. He taught that God is both just and justifier, making us righteous in Christ Jesus by His grace. Substitutionary atonement is a profound acknowledgment that God hates sin and evil, that He is right to judge it and that justice is as central to His nature as is love.

Why is all of this important? If we have a low view of God's anger and wrath, it means we have a low view of sin. In turn, that means we have a low view of the cross, the central event of the Christian faith. The cross is our hope for eternity. It is also our hope for all of humankind.

Both Testaments speak of God's justice and wrath, but certain voices in the church use the subject of wrath to try to distinguish the Father from the Son. When they read the Old Testament, they see God as an angry, vindictive Father; in the New Testament, they see the Son as a kinder version who has come to temper His dad's wrath and protect us from it. This portrayal flies in the face of Scripture. We know from the doctrine of the Trinity that the Father and Son are one and the same, having the same attitude toward sin and righteousness. As we will see also, the New Testament speaks of God's wrath from the gospels to Revelation.

The psalms themselves refute any distinction between God's justice and His love. The psalmist Asaph wrote that no sin escapes punishment and that all who sin will find God holding a cup of judgment. "For in the hand of the Lord there is a cup with foaming wine, well mixed, and he pours out from it, and all the wicked of the earth shall drain it down to the dregs" (Psalm 75:8). David knew this side of God, and he invoked it in his opening cry of Psalm 5. "O Lord, rebuke me not in your anger, nor discipline me in your wrath" (Psalm 5:1).

Even though David feared God's anger, he knew the Lord's assuring love equally well. In Psalm 23, he wrote famously of God's ability to transport his soul to green pastures and still waters. Here in Psalm 5, we see that David had an equally deep knowledge of God's justice. His fear of the Lord was a holy one based on what he knew of God's wrath toward evil. Weighing heavily in David's mind were truths that would later be expressed by the prophet Nahum. "The Lord is a jealous and avenging God; the Lord is avenging and wrathful; the Lord takes vengeance on his adversaries and keeps wrath for his enemies. The Lord is slow to anger and great in power, and the Lord will by no means clear the guilty . . . . Who can stand before his indignation? Who can endure the heat of his anger? His wrath is poured out like fire, and the rocks are broken into pieces by him" (Nahum 1:2-3,6).

Paul addressed this aspect of God's wrath. "For the wrath of God is revealed from heaven against all ungodliness and unrighteousness of men, who by their unrighteousness suppress the truth" (Romans 1:18). This verse holds a significant truth that many of us overlook. According to Paul, heaven isn't just about choirs and angels; heaven also reveals God's wrath. This is not something to be missed. We have known and tasted the Lord's all-encompassing love; therefore, we can know that any wrath from Him isn't bad or wrong. Like His love, it comes from the righteous hand of a merciful God.

David was clearly familiar with both God's love and God's justice, and he didn't compromise his view of either. In fact, I believe David's honest approach to his own sin made the difference in how the Lord responded to his repentance and to Saul's. Saul's faith kept moving downward on a self-centered trajectory, while David kept looking upward in his crises, reminding himself of God's righteous, merciful nature. This is instructive for us. Unless we face the depth of our sin honestly, recognizing how far our depravity causes us to fall, we won't enjoy the full measure of Christ's victory for us on the cross. What could be a source of rejoicing for us will become dead-letter, a paper doctrine.

This is important to grasp, because according to Paul, the fullness of God's judgment has yet to come. While His wrath is indeed revealed from Heaven, not everyone takes this seriously or soberly. To everyone with an indifferent heart, Paul wrote, "But because of your hard and impenitent heart you are storing up wrath for yourself on the day of wrath when God's righteous judgment will be revealed" (Romans 2:5). This describes the final cup of God's wrath to be poured out. On that day, the Lord will defeat death and triumph over evil, and He will judge all things righteously.

At the final judgment, Jesus, the Son, will deliver the wrath of heaven. Consider John's description of Jesus near the end of Revelation. "He is clothed in a robe dipped in blood, and the name by which he is called is The Word of God . . . From his mouth comes a sharp sword with which to strike down the nations, and he will rule them with a rod of iron. He will tread the winepress of the fury of the wrath of God the Almighty" (Revelation 19:13, 15). In this passage, Jesus, not the Father, is the one trampling down the grapes of wrath in the winepress to bring forth judgment.

The prophet Isaiah described an equally fearful vision when he saw Jesus. Notice how close its details are to John's description in Revelation. "Who is this who comes from Edom, in crimsoned garments from Bozrah, he who is splendid in his apparel, marching in the greatness of his strength? 'It is I, speaking in righteousness, mighty to save.' Why is your apparel red, and your garments like his who treads in the winepress? 'I have trodden the winepress alone, and from the peoples no one was with me; I trod them in my anger and trampled them in my wrath; their lifeblood spattered on my garments, and stained all my apparel. For the day of vengeance was in my heart, and my year of redemption had come'" (Isaiah 63:1-4).

What a terrifying description. Remember, Isaiah was the same writer who provided one of the Bible's warmest, most glorious portraits of Jesus alongside one of the best-known phrases about Him. " . . . I saw the Lord sitting upon a throne, high and lifted up; and the train of his robe filled the temple. Above him stood the seraphim . . . And one called to another and said: 'Holy, holy, holy is the LORD of hosts; the whole earth is full of his glory!'" (Isaiah 6:1-4).

These images of Christ—one terrifying, one glorious—do not conflict. Still, Isaiah didn't seem to recognize Jesus in chapter sixty-three. This blood-spattered figure didn't look like the one whose train filled the emple with glory. Isaiah literally had to ask, "Who is this?" The Lord had to explain to him, "It is I," meaning, "I'm the same Lord you worship with affection and love." The image in this scene is of a warrior fighting against wickedness, his sword drawn from its sheath to wipe out all evil coming against his kingdom.

A lot of voices in the church are asking the same question that Isaiah did. "Who are You? You can't possibly be God. The Lord we know would never act like this." Others in the church may ask, "Who are You?" as in, "I never knew You this way because I never understood Your justice before. I never grasped how seriously You take sin and rebellion."

Centuries before Isaiah, David showed a similar knowledge of God's righteous wrath against sin when he prayed, "O Lord, rebuke me not in your anger, nor discipline me in your wrath" (Psalm 6:1). He was saying, in essence, "Lord, I know you are a God of anger. Therefore, here is what I ask of you." "Turn, O Lord, deliver my life; save me for the sake of your steadfast love" (Psalm 6:4). David acknowledged, "Lord, I understand Your discipline. I get the need for Your rebuke. Please, just don't let Your discipline come from Your wrath, or I won't survive. Let it be from Your heart of mercy."

There is good news for us in David's cry. Like David, we know we deserve God's wrath and judgment. The cup of wrath we've examined here, though, is also one of power that leads to joy. How is this so? We see it in Christ's prayer in the Garden of Gethsemane just before He went to the cross. "And going a little farther he fell on his face and prayed, saying, 'My Father, if it be possible, let *this cup* pass from me; nevertheless, not as I will, but as you will'" (Matthew 26:39, my emphasis). What was the cup Jesus held in Gethsemane, the one He prayed would pass from Him? It was the same cup we've been talking about, the one filled with all the dregs of humanity's sins throughout history. This was the cup of wrath that was to be poured out on all wickedness and those who commit it.

Think of what Jesus was about to take on. He was going to bear the full justice of the righteous wrath aroused in God over every murder, every adultery, every act of greed, abuse, pride, and immorality ever committed and that would ever be committed. In other words, Jesus was holding death in His hands. By taking on the wrath of God over all evil, Jesus was going to bring freedom to those who could not bring it to themselves and that is all of us.

Deuteronomy 27 mentions all the terrible things that would befall those who chose not to walk in the Lord's ways. It literally says the people would bring a curse on themselves. Paul referred to this when he wrote of Jesus' sacrifice, "Christ redeemed us from the curse of the law by becoming a curse for us—for it is written, 'Cursed is everyone who is hanged on a tree'" (Galatians 3:13). Peter added to this, "He himself bore our sins in his body on the tree, that we might die to sin and live to righteousness. By his wounds you have been healed" (1 Peter 2:24). If you want to understand the awesome beauty and power of substitutionary atonement, you have to understand only one thing: Jesus took your place. Christ stands in the place of everyone who deserves God's righteous wrath over their depravity. He not only took our sins away but He incorporated His own righteousness into us. This is one of the most glorious doctrines in all of Scripture. Far from being cruel and abusive, it is the ultimate act of love.

That is the substitutionary aspect; the atonement aspect, or "at-one-ment," is the reality of being made one with God. No previous sacrifice could achieve that. No human act on our part, whether sorrow or repentance, could exchange our sin for God's righteousness. The only way any of us could ever be one with God was if the righteous penalty for our sin was paid in full by the perfect sacrifice. There was only One Who could pay that price, and that was Jesus, giving Himself up on the cross. Through His sacrificial act for us we have been given freedom, victory, and power to walk in the righteousness of God. "For our sake he made him to be sin who knew no sin, so that in him we might become the righteousness of God" (2 Corinthians 5:21). He has finished the work of this great exchange, our sin for His righteousness.

David could still foresee a day a coming that would be full of God's wrath. At the same time, he foresaw the cross. Indeed, the entire Old Testament points to it. I believe David might have been giving thanks ahead of time for that work when he wrote, "Turn, O Lord, deliver my life" (Psalm 6:4). He seemed to understand, "I don't merit it, but You can make me free." With this realization, all of a sudden, David's heart could leap in praise and exultation, "He has delivered me!" "Depart from me, all you workers of evil, for the Lord has heard the sound of my weeping. The Lord has heard my plea; the Lord accepts my prayer" (Psalm 6:8-9). I believe David's closing verse is an image of what happened at the cross for us all. "All my enemies shall be ashamed and greatly troubled; they shall turn back and be put to shame in a moment" (Psalm 6:10). All of David's sins and the curses that came with them—shame, fear, dread and sickness of soul—were put to flight.

Jesus did this for all of us at the cross. He took on the penalty we deserved and gave us freedom. We are to come to Him with our sins, no matter how awful they are, because His blood has already purchased our substitutionary atonement. We are no longer under God's righteous wrath, and we no longer bear guilt, shame, or condemnation. He has removed it all. All our existential dread is gone. Instead, we repent and face God's discipline willingly, knowing our prayer will be heard, just as David's was. "O Lord, rebuke me not in your anger, nor discipline me in your wrath. Be gracious to me, O Lord" (Psalm 6:1-2). His work is finished and complete, setting us on holy ground with nothing to hinder us from His plans and purpose.

CHAPTER SEVEN

Psalm 6 - Part II
The Holy Spirit's Healing Power

1 O Lord, rebuke me not in your anger,
  nor discipline me in your wrath.

2 Be gracious to me, O Lord, for I am languishing;
  heal me, O Lord, for my bones are troubled.

3 My soul also is greatly troubled.
  But you, O Lord—how long?

4 Turn, O Lord, deliver my life;
  save me for the sake of your steadfast love.

5 For in death there is no remembrance of you;
  in Sheol who will give you praise?

6 I am weary with my moaning;
  every night I flood my bed with tears;
  I drench my couch with my weeping.

7 My eye wastes away because of grief;
  it grows weak because of all my foes.

8 Depart from me, all you workers of evil,
  for the Lord has heard the sound of my weeping.

9 The Lord has heard my plea;
  the Lord accepts my prayer.

10 All my enemies shall be ashamed and greatly troubled;
  they shall turn back and be put to shame in a moment.

THIS CHAPTER CONTINUES OUR LOOK at Psalm 6. In the previous chapter, we didn't cover all the verses of this psalm, and embedded here is an important theme I'd like to highlight. It is the healing power of the Holy Spirit. We think of healing as a New Testament theme, but David's composing of Psalm 6 speaks directly to it.

These days, there isn't much talk in the church about the Holy Spirit's power to heal. We think of His work as mostly renewing our minds and hearts, but He also delivers us from sickness. In fact, when He touches us with physical healing, He transforms our lives. We rejoice in this because behind all of Jesus' wonders and the miraculous acts of the apostles is the core message of the gospel: God's love for humankind.

At the outset of Psalm 6, we read David's cry to be healed. In the previous chapter, we saw David concerned over past sins he had committed. In verse one, he wondered whether he would always be under God's wrath. At the same time, he grasped the grace and mercy of God through his repentance because he understood God's unmerited favor. David's condition had weakened him severely, and in verse two, he prayed for the Lord to have compassion on him. It is here we see David's appeal for healing. " . . . heal me, O Lord, for my bones are troubled" (Psalm 6:2). David's struggles went beyond wrestling over sin emotionally and intellectually. His body was in agonizing pain. He wrote, "I am weary with my moaning; every night I flood my bed with tears; I drench my couch with my weeping" (Psalm 6:6). Endless physical suffering can affect our mental condition, causing us to question where the Lord is while we are in pain. "My soul also is greatly troubled. But you, O Lord—how long?" (Psalm 6:3).

We have already seen David's fear of his enemies and of death. In verse eight he wrote, "Depart from me, all you workers of evil" (Psalm 6:8). He was saying, "Go away, all you workers of evil who've come to teal my life and vitality. May all my enemies be disgraced and terrified. May they turn back suddenly in shame." I believe physical sickness is one such enemy we face in life. So is death. When Jesus was on the earth, He turned back both of these enemies with the miracles He performed. In fact, throughout the gospels, as well as in other books of the New Testament, the word "immediately" is used to describe God's healings. A blind man was healed of his lifelong condition immediately. A demon-possessed child who threw himself into fires was delivered from his condition immediately. A woman who touched the hem of Jesus' garment was healed immediately after fourteen years of physical suffering.

Sickness and sorrows are part of life. We constantly live between two realms of conflict: the enemies that work against us and the glorious love of God that is for us and not against us. As a pastor, I long to see the Lord's healing power unleashed through His church. I pray to see His merciful love manifested in physical deliverances in our communities. I long to see His wonder-working power through simple, spoken words that send enemies fleeing and cause sickness to melt away. I want to see His church stand in faith that God actually does heal, that He's still in the miracle-working business, that His transforming love does not change but is the same yesterday, today, and forever. Every healing and deliverance is a demonstration of His merciful, unmerited love and a pushback against the enemy of our souls. All of these things were living realities in the early church.

When it comes to physical healing today, most of us wonder what God is up to in the world. There are two schools of thought concerning how and whether God heals today. The first is known as cessation theology. Cessationists believe that the supernatural gifts of the Spirit, including healing, ceased to exist at a certain point in time. They fully acknowledge the gifts of the Spirit as Paul outlined them in 1 Corinthians 12, 13 and 14 including gifts of prophecy, tongues, interpretation and healing. They acknowledge that these were fully operational among many people in the Bible from Jesus' disciples to the seventy-two others Jesus commissioned to preach and perform wonders, to the New Testament apostles and to many others including elders in the early churches.

According to cessationists, these works eventually ceased to exist, based on a passage in 1 Corinthians 13. "As for prophecies, they will pass away; as for tongues, they will cease; as for knowledge, it will pass away. For we know in part and we prophesy in part, but when the perfect comes, the partial will pass away" (1 Corinthians 13:8-10). To cessationists, the "perfect" referred to here is the written Bible. Once the biblical canon was finalized with its sixty-six books, there was no further need for "the partial," meaning demonstrations of signs and wonders. Until that time, God's people were given authority to lay hands on the sick, and they would recover. Once the Word of God arrived in its perfection, supernatural works became useless.

I think this doctrine reflects a poor understanding of Scripture. I believe the perfection Paul mentioned will happen only with Jesus' return. It would actually be strange for Paul to say that gifts would cease because in 1 Corinthians 14 he wrote about how churches are built up and thrive when the spiritual gifts are used to God's glory. He illustrated this by describing the evangelistic impact on any given stranger who would walk into a church and hear someone delivering a prophecy. The stranger would understand through the prophecy that God was speaking directly to his heart. "But if all prophesy, and an unbeliever or outsider enters, he is convicted by all, he is called to account by all, the secrets of his heart are disclosed, and so, falling on his face, he will worship God and declare that God is really among you" (1 Corinthians 14:24-25).

The second school of thought about the gifts of the Holy Spirit is that God continues to work wonders as He did throughout the Bible. To Paul, the supernatural gifts were a normal part of church life. He was always advocating for their use in both building up the church and demonstrating God's love to the lost. The spiritual gifts were truly good news not only to Paul's readers but to every church generation that has followed. Today, the message is simple and clear: We can pray not only for our own healing but for others', too.

David obviously didn't have this New Testament revelation, but he knew intuitively that the Lord was able to heal. He understood the character of the Lord so he cried out in naked honesty, "Oh, God, I am sick. My bones are wasting and in agony. Please, heal me!"

The psalms reveal many deep things about the Lord, but not until Jesus came to earth was God's nature fully expressed to humankind. His deity was revealed in the bodily form of the Son, and so Jesus said, "Whoever has seen me has seen the Father" (John 14:9). The author of Hebrews wrote that Jesus was the Father's exact representation on earth. He is the radiance of the glory of God and the exact imprint of his nature" (Hebrews 1:3). Paul wrote, "He is the image of the invisible God, the firstborn of all creation" (Colossians 1:15). He spoke also of "the riches of full assurance of understanding and the knowledge of God's mystery, which is Christ, in whom are hidden all the treasures of wisdom and knowledge" (Colossians 2:2-3). In short, we can know what God is like because Jesus is God.

The sending of the Son to earth was God's greatest demonstration of His love. When Christ's heart went out to the hungry and He fed them by the thousands, it was a direct expression of the Father's compassionate mercy. So were His healing deliverances. When He freed people from their illnesses, He revealed the heart behind the compassion so that we might believe in God to perform great acts for His glory.

I believe if we say today that God has ceased to perform wonders, we quench the Spirit. Any teacher ought to be careful about saying that God has ceased miraculous works. For one, to say this is to denounce the healing work that the Spirit is doing around the world right now. While thousands literally saw Jesus on earth touching the sick and healing them, scores of people today bear witness to compassionate wonders done in His name. God did not just heal a certain group of people in a certain time; He is healing. That is His nature. When David cried out, "Have compassion on me, Lord," he was speaking of something our forebears in the Old Testament longed to see: God's healing power through Christ's sacrifice on the cross. Isaiah prophesied, " . . . with his wounds we are healed" (Isaiah 53:5). Jesus' shed blood continues to heal our physical bodies as well as our souls.

As I wrote this chapter, I heard from some missionaries and other Christian leaders who are pastoring people in nationwide moves of God taking place in foreign countries. One who ministers in China told me that 50 percent of conversions there are the result of faith healings. These converts came to know Jesus either by what they experienced, witnessed or heard by reliable word of mouth. This amounts to millions of people who've come to Jesus through wonders performed by the Holy Spirit. Likewise, a leader in Nepal told me that 80 percent of all conversions there are due to miracles. Meanwhile, missiologists say that gospel impact in Iran is spreading by supernatural works of God. The rate of conversions among Iranians is the fastest-growing in the world, surpassing even that of China. Literally thousands of Iranians are coming to Christ on a continual basis and forming underground church groups.

As a minister of the gospel, I pray for the United States church to join in that flow. I don't want any doubt or fear to keep a Christian from praying for folks to be healed of sicknesses and debilitating conditions. I know that many believers' faith has shrunk because they haven't seen their prayers for healings answered. Too many of us allow such difficult experiences to cut us off from believing that God performs such works to reveal His glorious love. I pray for the Holy Spirit to infuse us all with renewed faith to see His love demonstrated through compassionate works of healing.

A core aspect of abundant life in Christ is vibrant faith. For that reason, Satan makes our faith his primary target. Jesus instructed, "The thief comes only to steal and kill and destroy. I came that they may have life and have it abundantly" (John 10:10). If the enemy can steal our faith and convince us that God can't trusted, it changes our whole belief system. We no longer look to the Lord to act. We may trust Him for rational truth but not for living truth such as the powerful truth that He heals.

David neared the edges of doubt in his own desperate cries to God. He pleaded, "If this sickness continues, my enemy is going to put me in the grave. Please, Lord, have compassion on me." Despite his many tribulations, David still knew God worked wonders. Through whatever ailments he faced, he trusted God's mercy to touch him with deliverance. "But you, O Lord—how long? Turn, O Lord, deliver my life" (Psalm 6:3-4). In other words, "God, I turn to You, but how long must I wait before You restore me? Don't let me languish, or through this endless suffering, my faith will fail."

In verse eight, David seemed to receive a revelation. After detailing his many pains in the first seven verses, David suddenly wrote, "Depart from me, all you workers of evil, for the LORD has heard the sound of my weeping" (Psalm 6:8). David seemed compelled to command all surrounding evildoers to flee from him. Why? He explained, "The Lord has heard my plea. Therefore, go away! All of you are going to be disgraced and terrified." This verse suggests to me that David may have been talking to himself as much as to his enemies. He might have been praying, "Go away, all unbelief. Go away, all cynicism and sarcasm that came to me through all my bitter experiences. Instead, come into me, faith and belief. Come in, all passion and desire."

The apostle John wrote, "The reason the Son of God appeared was to destroy the works of the devil" (1 John 3:8). What are the works of the devil? We have already seen that those works are to kill, steal and destroy. When we allow our faith to be stolen, succumbing to doubt, fear, and unbelief, we stop trusting God to do the awesome things He has already planned for us. We simply don't believe His interventions will ever happen again. That short-circuits the abundant life we are promised, and it cripples our calling to bring healing to others.

The belief that the gifts of the Holy Spirit have ceased isn't just poor theology. It is a belief with a very real effect. When John wrote that Jesus came to destroy the devil's works, he said in the same verse, "Whoever makes a practice of sinning is of the devil, for the devil has been sinning from the beginning" (1 John 3:8). Christ made clear that unbelief is sin, declaring this over and over in the gospels. The abundant life He promised is available to us only through faith. As James wrote, "The prayer of a righteous person has great power as it is working" (James 5:16).

Note what Paul wrote about the spiritual gift of healing. "And God has appointed in the church first apostles, second prophets, third teachers, then miracles, then gifts of healing, helping, administrating, and various kinds of tongues" (1 Corinthians 12:28). This is great news to all who are hurting, sick, and in pain. We can pray to be healed, and we can also pray for others to receive healing. "Is anyone among you sick? Let him call for

he elders of the church, and let them pray over him, anointing him with
il in the name of the Lord" (James 5:14). As the body of Christ, we are
o call for help from church elders who can pray for our healing. In turn,
ve are also called to bring His healing to others. Finally, we are called to
ring healing to the world, trusting God to demonstrate His good news
verywhere we go. Thus, Christ's works of healing didn't die out with the
welve disciples or with the seventy-two others He commissioned or with
he acts of the apostles. Jesus calls us to fulfill the same supernatural works
f mercy today.

The church is meant to be a supernatural church. The body of Christ
s not just doctrinal. It is a living organism. Yes, our doctrine needs to
e rich, fervent and vital; but it is brought alive by the Holy Spirit. That
appens through the supernatural power of God. Jesus demonstrated
his, speaking words of life accompanied by signs and wonders. Paul and
ther early church leaders did the same. The first-century church walked
n the supernatural, as did the second-century church, and Christ's body
as been doing the same for 2,000 years. In this way, the gospel is meant
not only for the lost but for the sick as well. The message of good news
accompanied by signs and wonders is meant to be taken outside the
church to a waiting world.

My wife and I committed to putting this conviction into practice.
Wherever we planned to go on any given day—to the grocery story, the
bank, the mall, a park or a restaurant—we prayed before leaving that the
Lord would set up divine appointments for us ahead of time. We trusted
Him to send us to folks who needed to hear His good news that He heals
and that they could experience His love for them. One day, our waiter at
a restaurant asked to excuse himself because he needed to go outside to
his car. He explained, "I'm in a lot of pain right now, and I have to go get

my pills for it." When he came back, we asked him about his condition and he described battling twenty-eight different maladies throughout his lifetime. We could tell this man had been through a lot. I asked if he would let us pray for him, and he looked amazed. "I have a friend who has been praying for me," he said. "In fact, that friend sent his pastor to my apartment to pray for me. Now here you are wanting to pray for me, too. Kelly and I took his hands and prayed for his healing.

As far as we know, no supernatural work of healing happened in that moment. We haven't seen him since then to be able to check on his health. What was clear to us, though, is that God is sending servants across this man's path to assure him of His care. That is the point of healings, by the way. They are demonstrations of God's all-surpassing love for us. The Lord orchestrates divine opportunities for us, and when we speak the Gospel to others, He accompanies our words with His power, demonstrating His good news with healing acts of love.

Embedded in Paul's chapters on the spiritual gifts is his renowned chapter on the transforming power of God's love. Without that love, all signs and wonders and supernatural works are empty of meaning. "If I speak in the tongues of men and of angels, but have not love, I am a noisy gong or a clanging cymbal. And if I have prophetic powers, and understand all mysteries and all knowledge, and if I have all faith, so as to remove mountains, but have not love, I am nothing. If I give away all I have, and if I deliver up my body to be burned, but have not love, I gain nothing" (1 Corinthians 13:1-3).

What the church needs most to fulfill the healing work of the Holy Spirit is a baptism of love. Otherwise, as Paul said, we're just clanging symbols, bringing noise to the world instead of peace and healing. When love is the driving force behind our works, the gifts of the Holy Spirit unction in fullness. Our prayer should be, "Lord, You have called us to pray for the sick, and to do that we need a baptism of Your love. You have called us to bring good news to the poor in spirit, and to do that we need to be baptized in Your love. We confess, we walk past 100 people a day and never think to share Your good news with them. We go to the gym and pump weights and never think about Your love for the person working out next to us. Wake us up, O Lord; we need the fire of Your Spirit to ignite Your gifts in us."

This kind of prayer is firmly grounded in Scripture. Paul urged Timothy to have hands laid on him to rekindle the gifts of God he had been given. In fact, we are all told to earnestly desire the spiritual gifts and above all to seek God's baptism of love for the effective working of those gifts. "But earnestly desire the higher gifts. And I will show you a still more excellent way . . . . So now faith, hope, and love abide, these three; but the greatest of these is love" (1 Corinthians 12:31; 13:13). I believe that all these passages make clear that the supernatural works happening in China, Nepal, and Iran can happen here in the United States and in the Western world. Like our brothers and sisters in those oppressive countries, we also should want to see powerful evangelism, healing, prophetic words, and signs and wonders fully at work in Christ's body, bringing hope to the lost and healing to the broken. Through a fresh touch of the Holy Spirit and a baptism of His love, the church will once again be ignited to the works God has preordained for us to do. "For we are his workmanship, created in Christ Jesus for good works, which God prepared beforehand, that we should walk in them" (Ephesians 2:10).

The tide can be turned in a broken world when we trust the Holy Spirit to work His powerful healing through Christ's body. If we fall back on programs and projects to see Christ's gospel at work in the world, we won't witness the power that's needed to reach lost hearts and transform lives. If we rely solely on doctrine to fulfill our calling in Christ, we will have fallen short. We need to see the Holy Spirit move with power through His church.

If you are sick in body and heart as David was, or you know someone who is, you definitely need more than projects and programs. This chapter is your divine appointment. It is a call-out for you to believe again, to know that you can be healed, that God has called church leaders to pray for you, that He has healing power to give you so that you can lay your hands on suffering friends and pray for their restoration of body, heart, and mind. Indeed, this is the gospel Christ has called us to. We ought to long to see His presence move in power so that those who don't know Him will say, "God truly is in your midst" and will turn to Him in repentance and hope.

Pray for a fresh baptism of love. Let the Holy Spirit fall on you so that you may see those around you through Jesus' eyes and act as His hands and feet to set them free. He has passed His supernatural works onto us. Therefore, earnestly desire the spiritual gifts, so that you may be effective in speaking the gospel and bringing healing to those around you. Through His merciful love, may those you reach have their eyes opened to His amazing reality.

CHAPTER EIGHT

Psalm 7
Overcoming Accusations and Wounds

1 O Lord my God, in you do I take refuge;

    save me from all my pursuers and deliver me,

2 lest like a lion they tear my soul apart,

    rending it in pieces, with none to deliver.

3 O Lord my God, if I have done this,

    if there is wrong in my hands,

4 if I have repaid my friend with evil

    or plundered my enemy without cause,

5 let the enemy pursue my soul and overtake it,

    and let him trample my life to the ground

    and lay my glory in the dust. Selah

6 Arise, O Lord, in your anger;

    lift yourself up against the fury of my enemies;

    awake for me; you have appointed a judgment.

7 Let the assembly of the peoples be gathered about you;

    over it return on high.

8 The Lord judges the peoples;

    judge me, O Lord, according to my righteousness

    and according to the integrity that is in me.

9 Oh, let the evil of the wicked come to an end,

and may you establish the righteous—

you who test the minds and hearts,

O righteous God!

10 My shield is with God,

who saves the upright in heart.

11 God is a righteous judge,

and a God who feels indignation every day.

12 If a man does not repent, God will whet his sword;

he has bent and readied his bow;

13 he has prepared for him his deadly weapons,

making his arrows fiery shafts.

14 Behold, the wicked man conceives evil

and is pregnant with mischief

and gives birth to lies.

15 He makes a pit, digging it out,

and falls into the hole that he has made.

16 His mischief returns upon his own head,

and on his own skull his violence descends.

17 I will give to the Lord the thanks due to his righteousness,

and I will sing praise to the name of the Lord, the Most High.

LET'S REVIEW WHAT WE'VE READ to this point in the first six psalms. The psalter opens with a pronounced blessing in Psalm 1. After that, we see a lot of turmoil. Psalms 2 through 6 speak of nations raging against God and leaders plotting vain things; of trials, struggles, difficulties, and tribulations; and of needing relief for distress, sorrow, and grief. In short, the Psalms relate to the hardest things we face in life. It's a book that gives is words for our struggles. It shows us we can bring to God all our pain and griefs with prayers we can hold onto to face what we're going through.

This brings us to Psalm 7. This psalm was by David, and in it his struggles continued. Up to that point he had confessed his struggles, but in this psalm, he switched gears. He moved from physical trials to an emotional one, focusing on the heartache of his soul. This becomes clear even before we read verse one, in the heading that appears above the psalm, "A Shiggaion of David, which he sang to the Lord concerning the words of Cush, a Benjaminite." A shiggaion is "a lyrical poem composed under strong mental emotion," according to Easton's Bible Dictionary. Right away in the heading, we see that an enemy was speaking against David, using lies and accusations to destroy his reputation. The heading even names this enemy, Cush the Benjamite. How did David deal with Cush's accusing words? His response was this psalm, an anguished yet beautiful and prayerful song filled with harsh images reflecting David's emotions. "O Lord my God, in you do I take refuge; save me from all my pursuers and deliver me, lest like a lion they tear my soul apart, rending it in pieces, with none to deliver" (Psalm 7:1-2).

Those two verses reveal the framework for all that will appear in the following fifteen verses of the psalm. The main theme is accusations that tear at our souls. I believe this psalm is meant to help us overcome the wounds of an accuser, whether that is Satan or someone who opposes us. Lies tear at our soul like nothing else in life, and this psalm encourages us that the Lord raises up a standard against them.

This was the case with David. He had fought off bears and lions, battled giants and kings, and faced hostile armies and internal rebellions, yet rarely do we see him as distraught as he appeared in this psalm. He was under great duress, in pain and burdened with a deep, anguished sorrow of soul. Outwardly, he had vanquished mighty nations that came against him, but this internal battle was something different. His enemies in this conflict were words, and his warfare was one of the mind. David knew he was a sinner, yet his identity was one of integrity and righteousness, and for that reason, the accusations against him cut to his core.

David's struggle speaks to anyone who has been overcome by false words spoken against them. It may seem like a small thing for a seasoned warrior to be so concerned about mere words. In reality, though, this is the type of attack that overwhelms many of us, preoccupying our thoughts and nagging throughout the day. In fact, that is the very intent of such accusations. They're meant to hurt, harm, and haunt us. Such words fly like flaming arrows, piercing to the deepest level to drain us of all vitality. The accusations against David sent him spiraling into depression, confusion, fear, and discouragement. In this case, they were meant to bring down not just a man but a kingdom. David was promised by God that his kingdom would endure for generations, and David felt responsible for that. Now, however, he was a king without a throne.

Some commentaries speculate that Cush the Benjamite was an ally of Saul. Because he was from the Saul's tribe, Cush might even have been a relative. That would have made his accusations all the more painful to David because of David's unswerving loyalty to Saul. David's deepest trouble wasn't the militias that pursued him, chasing him into the hills where he had to hide among rocks and caves. His trouble was the widespread accusations by someone close to the king whom David served loyally. David's description of his pain in this psalm was vivid. He said it was like being torn apart by a lion. As a young shepherd, he would have seen up close the ferocity of lion attacks on the sheep he protected. He witnessed sharp teeth crushing their prey and claws ripping apart the orso. The image is of hopeless vulnerability, beyond any ability to survive. David wrote, "Nothing can deliver me when my soul is torn apart like this."

In the current culture, harmful accusations move fast and furiously through social media. Some of us have hurtful words thrown at us every day. All you need to do is post a picture on social media, and comments quickly pour in. It doesn't matter if you get 100 positive responses; the one that sticks with you is the hurtful one. This type of pain doesn't compare to what David went through, a man deposed from his kingdom and running for his life, but the harm caused by hurtful words do go beyond the psychological to the physical. It has been scientifically proven that one "thumbs down" on a Facebook post triggers a chemical reaction in the brain as if a physical assault has occurred. Social media's increasingly mean-spirited, cruel, thoughtless, purposefully painful words create something palpably negative in our lives. At its worst, this has driven some people, especially young people, to take their own lives.

Over the years, studies have shown brain images of people who went through painful experiences such as divorce or other rejections. The images were revealing. They were nearly identical to those of people who felt the physical pain of holding their hand over a hot surface. The chemical reaction in the brain was the same. It showed that emotional wounds release signals in the body the same way physical wounds do. Our bodies process both kinds of pain in remarkably similar ways.

I remember reading a book by a woman who had been verbally abused as a child. She said she wished she'd been physically wounded instead so that people could actually see the scars she bore throughout her life. Maybe then people would ask me what happened and understand the pain I carry," she said.

This is why David, and you and I, bring our wounds to the Lord. If we don't, if we try to bear them alone, the harm done to our soul by our accuser keeps chipping year after year. I think of one of my sons, who has the physique of an Olympic gymnast. He's in the best condition of anyone I've ever known. As it turned out, his conditioning was his compensation for something that happened to him in elementary school. He was slightly overweight then, and he was mocked by classmates who poked his belly and called him names. That ignited his anger, and he got into fight after fight. My wife and I never knew about this until years later when he was an adult. Hearing him talk about it ignited an anger in me and grieved me deeply as a father.

We've all had harmful words spoken over us. Sadly, this comes primarily from those closest to us, maybe a father who was neglectful or a mother who was abusive. It also comes from teachers, peers and even pastors. The message is "You'll never be good enough," or "You'll never make it," or "You're not worth it, so I'm leaving you." These words don't just bounce off us or disappear. They work their way into our self-image and rise up in our mind again and again. We tell ourselves, "They're right. This is who I am. What they say about my faults is accurate." We need the wisdom of the Holy Spirit to understand what is correct about us and what is a lie. We need to discern the difference between what we should own about ourselves and grow from it, and what is just damaging. We should be able to tell ourselves, "Yes, I need to change this aspect of my life," rather than, "I'm just this way, and I'm destined for failure." Above all, we need to know in the moment when a negative comment comes from an enemy who means to drag us to the ground and tear our soul apart.

Attacks against our character are a fact of life, and we need the Spirit's presence to face them. This is a spiritual battle. Paul desired "that we would not be outwitted by Satan; for we are not ignorant of his designs" (2 Corinthians 2:11). How exactly does the enemy try to take advantage of us? The prophet Zechariah was given a powerful vision of how Satan works. "Then he showed me Joshua the high priest standing before the angel of the Lord, and Satan standing at his right hand to accuse him" (Zechariah 3:1). We can imagine how this all went down. The Lord might have said to Joshua, "I have made you holy," to which the devil would blurt, "No, you can never be right with God!" The tension of this spiritual battle is something Christians go through every day. In fact, often when we're in the Lord's presence, the enemy jumps in with his hardest attacks. In such moments we're to summon the courage to say, "I'm going to listen to what the Lord says, not to this liar."

Jesus said of the devil, "He was a murderer from the beginning, and does not stand in the truth, because there is no truth in him. When he lies, he speaks out of his own character, for he is a liar and the father of lies" (John 8:44). This description is instructive to us in a crucial way. In short, if we hear an accusation from the enemy, we can know the opposite is true because he tells only lies.

What did David do with such accusations? His first act was to personalize his relationship with the Lord. He opened this psalm by calling out to God, "O Lord my God, in you do I take refuge" (Psalm 7:1). David was addressing a God who is personal, not some random entity in the universe. He was declaring, in essence, "The Lord is high and lofty, but he is also right here with me." His request was also deeply personal. " . . . save me from all my pursuers and deliver me" (Psalm 7:1). He wrote this with urgency, because in the very next verse he asked God to shut the jaws of a fearsome lion. " . . . lest like a lion they tear my soul apart, rending it in pieces, with none to deliver" (Psalm 7:2). David could make his request this personal because he knew God's character and nature, that the Lord was both a strong tower and refuge. As a whole, this psalm is about God's righteousness, holiness, truthfulness, and omnipotence. For David, to know the Lord was to know security, peace, overcoming, and triumph. By knowing God's attributes and voice, David was able to discern the accusing voice of his enemy, and he would not believe the accusations. His psalm wasn't some letter confronting an enemy, or an appeal to an earthly judge, or a trumpet call to his military to come to his side; it was simply a song about God. In writing it, David was singing away his pains, sorrows, struggles, and wounds, presenting them all to the Lord. We can do the same. In addition, the New Testament tells us we have been given something more for such trying times. Paul wrote, "Likewise the Spirit helps us in our weakness. For we do not know what to pray for as we ought, but the Spirit himself intercedes for us with groanings too deep for words. And he who searches hearts knows what is the mind of the Spirit, because the Spirit intercedes for the saints according to the will of God" (Romans 8:26-27). What exactly are the "groanings too deep for words" Paul is talking about here?

Some call this singing in the Spirit. It's simply giving voice wordlessly to something that our mind might not be able to fully express. Sometimes when false, cruel words are formed against us, the anguish we feel can be so deep as to be inexplicable. In those instances, we can sing to the Lord by relying on the Spirit. These Spirit-led utterances are a form of combat, fighting demonic elements through God's power and not our own. What a merciful gift from the Lord. At times, we are able to pray with full understanding, and then in harder times we may also sing in the spirit beyond all understanding. The world has nothing like this gift to offer us. When our souls are being torn apart by lies, the Helper, the Holy Spirit, delivers us.

In verse three, David made a shift, opening his heart to God about whether he had committed the wrongs he was accused of. We have already talked in earlier chapters about David's terrible sins. Those sins were devious, deceptive, violent, and troubling. Yet David understood that he was forgiven of them. When everything was revealed and David confessed, the prophet Nathan assured him, "The Lord also has put away your sin; you shall not die" (2 Samuel 12:13). With this forgiveness in mind, David now sought to be justified by the Lord before his accuser. "O Lord my God, if I have done this, if there is wrong in my hands, if I have repaid my friend with evil or plundered my enemy without cause, let the enemy pursue my soul and overtake it, and let him trample my life to the ground and lay my glory in the dust" (Psalm 7:3-5). In other words, "Lord, if I did what my enemy says, then I deserve to be decimated by him. Let that happen if I'm guilty."

If you're a liar and somebody calls you that, it's hard for you to seek justification. You might feel too ashamed or embarrassed. When someone speaks the truth about your unrepented sins, however, the pain you feel isn't really a wound. It's more like piercing conviction. True pain comes when the accusations against us are false and unjustified, lies meant to do harm. This is why David was compelled to ask, "Lord, did I repay my friends' love with evil? Did I take advantage of my enemy without a cause?" Some scholars say David's second question here may have an alternative translation. The Hebrew phrase for "plundered my enemy" could be read as "equipped my enemy." In essence, the accusation was that David betrayed his friends and befriended his enemies. For David, who was the picture of loyalty, to even hint that he would betray Saul and his own nation would have crushed his heart. This was how the accuser wounded David to the core. Satan doesn't always attack our weaknesses. More often, he attacks our strengths. One of David's strengths was his love for people, and the people he ruled over sensed his genuine love for them. David also had a love for righteousness and truth. Therefore, Cush's accusation would have pierced David on two levels, first by questioning his loyalty and second by using an outright lie to do it.

Next time you're under attack, take a moment to see if it's in an area of strength for you. Maybe you have a deep love for people but someone has accused you of being unkind. My counsel to you is to not shrink back in defensiveness. Rather, continue to be strong in that area. God has a part for you to play in His kingdom; and if you turn your focus to the attack, you'll be sidelined from your holy calling. That's the enemy's strategy, to derail you from your role in the powerful work of the Spirit.

David remained loyal to Saul even when the king was determined to kill him. Scripture tells us David had opportunities to kill Saul, and it's clear he would have been justified in following through. Instead, David defended his attacker even when his fellow soldiers wanted to kill Saul. This fierce loyalty in David is precisely what Cush was attacking. It caused David his deepest anguish, because the accusations called into question the very core of his identity. In utter frustration, David cried out to the Lord, "If I am guilty of any of this, then let my accusers crush my reputation. Let them take my honor and integrity. Let them shout from the housetops that I'm a traitor. If any of it is true, I'll acknowledge my guilt."

You may wonder how David could so boldly seek to justify himself when he clearly wasn't an innocent man in all matters. David didn't claim to be blameless in everything but only in the things of which he was accused. Ultimately, his boldness was based on his confidence in God's cleansing of his sin. David had repented and been forgiven, and his integrity was restored. Thus, he could say, as he did in verse eight, "The Lord judges the peoples; judge me, O Lord, according to my righteousness and according to he integrity that is in me" (Psalm 7:8). In fact, David is our example when we're under attack from lies. We shouldn't succumb to any accusations, bemoaning, "Yes, I deserve this because I'm a sinner." Sadly, we often agree more with what our enemy says about us than with what our Savior says. The Bible makes clear that we are bought, forgiven, and cleansed by Christ. This gives us integrity to speak with boldness as David did.

Christ has gifted us with three antidotes for the times we face attacks of accusation. The first antidote we're given is a clean conscience. We obtain this through repentance, as we turn from sin and seek God's forgiveness. Instead of wallowing in guilt over our sins, we have to accept that Christ cleanses us of them. He restores us to wholeness, and we never have to listen to any accusation about that sin again.

The second antidote to soul-tearing words is to know our identity in Christ. We reject the enemy's lies when we declare, "This is who I am, saved and redeemed by Jesus." We obtain confidence for this by understanding the Word of God.

The third antidote to attacks through lies is to confess our righteousness. David did this, praying, "Lord, these lies are tearing my soul apart, but I stand on integrity." He wasn't saying, "Look how perfect I am," but rather, Look at what God has done in me. I have sinned but He has forgiven me. He healed me when I was lost. Now watch Him defend me from false accusations. The Lord is my deliverer!"

Consider the effect of these three antidotes on David. At that point in the psalm, he prayed with the boldness of Elijah. "Arise, O Lord, in your anger; lift yourself up against the fury of my enemies; awake for me; you have appointed a judgment" (Psalm 7:6). This wasn't just a wishful prayer on the part of a man wracked with guilt. David's confident faith was based on the Lord's righteousness. As James wrote, "The prayer of a righteous person has great power as it is working" (James 5:16). It doesn't matter how "bad" or "good" our walk is on any given day. When we turn from our sin in repentance, He makes us righteous, and we stand sanctified, pure, and filled with the Holy Spirit. Then we can pray with the boldness of lions. When David finally rose up, it was with the boldness of God, calling for every demonic action against him to cease.

In verse six, David asked the Lord to do three things on his behalf: (1) to be angry over his situation, (2) to rise up against his enemies and (3) to "awake" bringing righteous judgment. Note that all three of these things denote ascendence. The picture is of God being roused by injustice, rising up to do battle and delivering His beloved servant from all accusations. By reminding himself of God's incredible nature, David envisioned the Lord bringing justice to his cause before all the people of God. "Let the assembly of the peoples be gathered about you; over it return on high" (Psalm 7:7). He asked the Lord to let everyone see justice done as if in a courtroom. "The Lord judges the peoples; judge me, O LORD, according to my righteousness and according to the integrity that is in me" (Psalm 7:8).

In this scenario, David pictures God overhearing truth and lies, discerning and judging. So David made his plea like a lawyer. "Oh, let the evil of the wicked come to an end, and may you establish the righteous— you who test the minds and hearts, O righteous God!" (Psalm 7:9). David was calling on God for action. He said the Lord will not only awaken to decree what is right and wrong; He will also pronounce a judgment and move to act on it. "If a man does not repent, God will whet his sword; he has bent and readied his bow; he has prepared for him his deadly weapons, making his arrows fiery shafts" (Psalm 7:12-13). There is no greater image of God doing battle for us than this one. David was saying, "The righteous judge will bring this verbal abuse to an end. He has brought weapons to shut the mouth of the fearsome lion and silence his accusing lies."

What a powerful picture David painted for us to be able to face our trials. The Lord is present with us not just to comfort us in our suffering. He also wields a mighty sword to silence the lies brought against us. God does this so commandingly that we no longer believe the enemy's lies about us. What a mighty and merciful deliverer we have. We can rest knowing that the Lord is not just a God of words but of actions. He delivers us from harm by fighting that battle for us.

In verse ten, David dropped a curious statement. "My shield is with God, who saves the upright in heart" (Psalm 7:10). The translation here is actually, "My shield is on God." In David's eyes, God wasn't surrounding him as a kind of force field, the way we often picture Him doing. Rather, David pictured himself handing over his shield to God to do the work of protecting him. He stated, in essence, "My shield is in the Lord's hands, and I abide in Him. He is my fierce warrior, strong tower, and righteous strength, so when the enemy tries to attack me, he's not coming against me but against God." This kind of enemy attack will go nowhere. In fact, as we will see, it falls back on the attacker.

In the church today, we don't hear much about God as a judge with great indignation. Most teaching about Jesus' character revolves around His meekness and gentleness, and that is absolutely true about Him. Yet every day, God is indignant over the injustices of the world, His fierce anger stirred up. In response, He prepares His bow and sword as if going to war intent to bring judgment on all wickedness. I identify with this kind of indignation and fierceness, and you may, too, on a deeply personal level. It's what I felt as I listened to my adult son tell his story of being bullied in school.

At this point in Psalm 7, we see an odd twist occur. Instead of describing a massive quashing of enemies by God, David described something else "Behold, the wicked man conceives evil and is pregnant with mischief and gives birth to lies. He makes a pit, digging it out, and falls into the hole that he has made" (Psalm 7:14-15). To me, these verses are like a scene from a movie that's both a comedy and a tragedy. An evil person digs a pit for the righteous to fall in, but instead he falls in himself and is buried. "His mischief returns upon his own head, and on his own skull his violence descends" (Psalm 7:16). The message is clear: The wicked bring judgment upon themselves. This is what happened to the evil Haman in the Book of Esther. He built a gallows to hang Esther's uncle, Mordecai, whom Haman had condemned with lies. When Haman's evil plot was uncovered, however, he was hanged on the very gallows he had built for another man.

David began his psalm with a wound, but his conclusion was quite different. Sometimes in the depths of our sorrows we sing ourselves to sleep with tears. Our song may be one of wounds, depression, sorrows or discouragement. Maybe we've been falsely accused as David was. If any of this describes you, I encourage you to take a page from Psalm 7. David shifted his cry of anguish to focus on the nature and character of God. That is when his wound began to heal. The same antidote is available to us. As we ponder the incredible attributes of the Lord and His amazing love for us, we regain faith. Our worries begin to flee and we gather confidence as we recount our redemptive history with the Lord. Hurtful memories start to heal as we consider His merciful love, and new words come into our song: "The Lord is righteous, strong, and powerful. Christ has overcome the world, and I hide myself in Him."

David's song shifted from fear and anguish to praise. "I will give to the Lord the thanks due to his righteousness, and I will sing praise to the name f the Lord, the Most High" (Psalm 7:17). He rekindled his faith by reflecting n the Lord's goodness despite his difficulties. "I know Who God is. He is or me, not against me. Why should I worry about enemies when I know ny redeemer lives?" The best cure for our crisis is in knowing the Lord and ow He works in the world. When we shift our focus to Him, He turns ur trembling into thanksgiving, our fear into faith, and our wounds into vorship. We can say to any accuser, "You may say this about me, but God ays differently. I will listen to Him, not to your lie. You think your words vill destroy me, but the Lord is my faithful deliverer. You're a liar while He s always true."

Our accuser flees, and we walk on in confidence with a song of praise n our lips. We are forgiven, washed and beloved, knowing He loves us, ares for us, and chooses us. We are protected by the great and mighty King. That is who we are in Christ.

CHAPTER NINE

Psalm 8

God Loves Using Small Things

To the choirmaster: according to The Gittith. A Psalm of David.

1 O Lord, our Lord,

   how majestic is your name in all the earth!

You have set your glory above the heavens.

2   Out of the mouth of babies and infants,

you have established strength because of your foes,

   to still the enemy and the avenger.

3 When I look at your heavens, the work of your fingers,

   the moon and the stars, which you have set in place,

4 what is man that you are mindful of him,

   and the son of man that you care for him?

5 Yet you have made him a little lower than the heavenly beings

   and crowned him with glory and honor.

6 You have given him dominion over the works of your hands;

   you have put all things under his feet,

7 all sheep and oxen,

   and also the beasts of the field,

8 the birds of the heavens, and the fish of the sea,

   whatever passes along the paths of the seas.

9 O Lord, our Lord,

   how majestic is your name in all the earth!

TO TAKE IN PSALM 8, it is best to view it in the context of the seven psalms preceding it. Throughout those psalms, David described the anguish of his heart. He dealt with trials, tribulations, sorrows, and sufferings as well as issues of sin in his life. He faced persecution and adversaries that sometimes came from within his own family. He dealt with sickness and bodily suffering. In short, he went through almost every type of human crisis we could imagine.

You may understand some of what David went through. If you're dealing with marital struggles, financial problems or a frightening diagnosis, you understand some of the emotional upheaval he experienced. He had external troubles all around but also endured fierce internal battles with doubt, fear, and unbelief. He questioned God, asking in essence, "Lord, how long will this last? How much do You expect me to take before I'm overwhelmed by my enemies?" Can you relate to this? I certainly can. Scripture says David had a heart after God, yet he was plagued by doubt because of his many trials. Satan took advantage of David's vulnerable state and does the same with us today. When we're assailed by constant difficulties, the devil accuses us, "Look at how little faith you have. This is all happening because of your unbelief. You don't trust God at all." David was a true servant who continually sought to please God, yet through the first seven psalms we see him struggling fiercely. In Psalm 8, however, David made a bold statement that put all his anguished expression in perspective. Through his writing, I hear the Lord telling us, "Give ear to My servant's message here. It expresses a desperate, hungry heart in a different way than you have seen."

The first seven psalms follow a similar pattern. The pattern we see in the early psalms develop from the heart-cries of a man known to us as a man after God's heart. "He raised up David to be their king, of whom he estified and said, 'I have found in David the son of Jesse a man after my heart, who will do all my will'" (Acts 13:22). Despite these descriptions of David, he seemed to wake up downcast every morning rather than joyful. His first thought was of the battles he had to face. Maybe his dreams were restless or even frightening. He probably spent sleepless hours going over his difficulties, wondering how he might solve them, what he did to deserve them or how his own sin might have caused them. "I am weary with my moaning; every night I flood my bed with tears; I drench my couch with my weeping" (Psalm 6:6).

Think about all that was on David's mind. In Psalm 2, he asked, "Why do the nations rage? Why do the people imagine vain things?" In Psalm 3, he asked, "How many are my foes? Many have risen up against me." In Psalm 4, he pleaded, "Answer when I call, Lord. Give me relief from my distress." In Psalm 5, he prayed, "Consider my groan, God, and give attention to my cry." In Psalm 6, he asked, "Lord, don't rebuke me in Your anger. Don't discipline me in Your wrath." In Psalm 7, he cried, "Lord, You're my refuge. Save me from all my pursuers." In each of these, David began his conversations with God in a negative state. Many of us can understand that. When we're going through a heavy struggle, it's hard to approach the Lord with a joyful song in our heart. We know His joy exists somewhere deep down within our being, but it's obscured by the trials and tribulations of life.

Psalm 8 reflects the fact that all of us, no matter how trying our circumstances, still have joy underneath our worries. Maybe on the day that David composed Psalm 8, he woke plagued by the same negative thoughts. This time, however, as he considered his troubles, perhaps a memory shifted his thinking. He might have recalled the many times he was rescued from deep trouble. David knew those deliverances were due solely to the Lord's faithful care. Suddenly, David summoned a confidence that he would be delivered yet again. I picture him praying, "Lord, I often wonder, 'How long until You deliver me?' Yet I know I will be delivered. You have done it for me so many times."

We see this attitude reflected in the conclusion of every psalm so far. He ended Psalm 2, "Blessed are those who take refuge in the Lord." The final verse of Psalm 3 reads, "Salvation belongs to the Lord. Your blessing be upon your people." Psalm 4 ends on a note of peace: "I lie down and sleep, for you alone are Lord. You make me dwell in safety." Psalm 5 ends, "For you bless the righteous, O Lord, you cover him with favor as a shield." Psalm 6 concludes, "All my enemies shall be ashamed and greatly troubled. They shall be turned back." Psalm 7 is a kind of capstone to all this, in which David described his enemy's fate and then gave praise to God. "His mischief returns upon his own head, and on his own skull his violence descends. I will give to the Lord thanks due to his righteousness, and I will sing praise to the name of the Lord, the Most High" (Psalm 7:16-17).

It's as if after seven rounds of crying out his misery, David saw the pattern and woke to the deep reality of God's faithfulness. Alternatively maybe this psalm appears in the eighth position for a different reason. Perhaps the assemblers of the psalter recognized the completeness of the cycle of Psalms 1-7 and put Psalm 8 next in line because it offers only thanksgiving to God. "O Lord, our Lord, how majestic is your name in all the earth! You have set your glory above the heavens" (Psalm 8:1).

Psalm 8 is a powerful demonstration of how our deepest cries of anguish can be turned into the highest of praises. When we accept that the Lord fights our battles, our downcast spirit can be raised to a place of adoration and praise. Our thanksgiving to Him actually builds hope and confidence because it anchors us in the truth of His loving faithfulness. This sparks faith as we realize, "God is due my praise. I owe it to Him because He has

een with me in all my ups and downs. I have faced nothing alone, and no
nemy has triumphed over me. He triumphs over them! The Lord is right
n all He does, and He is right to allow my trials. I'm able to trust that good
hings are happening even as I undergo all these difficulties. Therefore, I
vill sing praises to the most high God. My problems aren't most high. My
motions about my crises are not most high. My dilemmas and difficulties
re not most high. Only one thing is most high, and that is the almighty
ord. He is most high over everything!" As soon as David resolved this in
is heart, it became a foundational truth for him.

What a huge difference it makes when we recognize, "God is a shield
bout me through everything. That is just a fact, and it holds true even
f my never-ending trial has me downcast. I may feel low about my
ircumstances, but God is most high over all of it."

This realization released David to write a different type of psalm.
ndeed, in Psalm 8 we see a radically different shift. It was the first psalm
n which David didn't start off describing a problem. Instead, he described
he Lord's glory, majesty, splendor, and power. Psalm 8 reflects a high view
of God yet also a God who is near to us in the low places of our problems.
Time after time, the Lord showed Himself strong on David's behalf, and
hat made David's problems seem smaller. God does the same for us.

God is bigger than we could ever get our minds around, and His
omnipotence is far beyond what our finite minds can imagine. When we
understand that God's infinite power is at work in our lives, we may find
springing forth from our heart a powerful song of rejoicing. That is Psalm
8 in a nutshell. It is the song of a lover of God who finally came to terms
with the fact that the Lord triumphs over our battles, and that made him
want to worship. Consider how differently David opened this psalm as
compared to those that precede it. "O Lord, our Lord, how majestic is your

name in all the earth! You have set your glory above the heavens. Out of the mouth of babies and infants, you have established strength because of your foes, to still the enemy and the avenger. When I look at your heavens, the work of your fingers, the moon and the stars, which you have set in place, what is man that you are mindful of him, and the son of man that you care for him? Yet you have made him a little lower than the heavenly beings and crowned him with glory and honor" (Psalm 8:1-5).

According to David, we are lower than the angels, yet we have been crowned with God's glory. Moreover, the Lord has given us dominion over all of creation. "You have given him dominion over the works of your hands; you have put all things under his feet, all sheep and oxen, and also the beasts of the field, the birds of the heavens, and the fish of the sea, whatever passes along the paths of the seas" (Psalm 8:6-8). David concluded this glory-filled psalm with simple praise. "O Lord, our Lord, how majestic is your name in all the earth!" (Psalm 8:9). What a dramatic shift this is in David's thinking. He placed the Lord's majesty and splendor above everything else. That is significant. Considering all the trials David faced, Psalm 8 was a bold statement of faith.

Early Jewish rabbis recognized that the declarations of this psalm could also be understood as questions, as though David were asking, for example, 'How majestic is Your name in all the earth?'" Midrash developed in ancient times as the way rabbis taught their students a disciplined approach to the Scriptures. One such approach to Psalm 8 was to see in it several declarations about God and to frame them as questions. This approach offers an awe-inspiring perspective, because the questions show God to be even more majestic in what He does for us.

Many of us tend to think of ourselves as insignificant, powerless, and ineffective in a vast and complex world. According to Psalm 8, however, e are God's crowning glory with dominion over all creation. On top f this, the Lord has endued us with power to accomplish His eternal urposes. He has given us gifts, skills, relationships and the infilling of [is Spirit to co-labor with Him to see His kingdom come on earth as it ; in Heaven.

You'll notice that some of the declarations in Psalm 8 were already ormed as questions. " . . . what is man that you are mindful of him, and he son of man that you care for him?" (Psalm 8:4). Framed as a question, his is as if David said, "This is too good to be true. God crowned us with lis glory and then gave us dominion over all things—how can it be? This s overwhelming, too astounding to grasp."

I love another declaration here that may be reshaped as a question. . . . how majestic is your name in all the earth!" (Psalm 8:9). David was aying, "Your majesty is indescribable, unmeasurable, and infallible. It s beyond anything we could think or imagine. The whole earth can't ontain it!" Let's apply what David said here to the way we picture God. Ve believe the Lord can do some things in our lives but not others, which n our minds puts Him in a very small box. When our prayer requests tren't answered as we wish, we complain, "God, You aren't there for ne." We diminish Him rather than acknowledge His omniscience in the ncredible ways He orchestrates our lives.

As a minister, I feel that the holy calling burning in my soul is to present God as big as the human mind can possibly comprehend. This kind of comprehension is a discipline. If you've ever looked through the wrong end of a telescope, you see things diminished from their reality. I pelieve this describes a large percentage of our thinking about God. By contrast, if you turn the telescope around, you get a bigger glimpse of reality than you could ever conceive on your own. Through Scripture and the revelation of the Holy Spirit our capacity to understand the Lord's ways is increased. He is always bigger than we could ever grasp, and His amazing workings are beyond us. The kind of awe-filled perspective I'm talking about ought to build our faith in Him rather than diminish it.

On the surface, it may seem like an irony that David's reverence was the result of all the difficulties and suffering he had been through. It wasn't trials that caused the shift in David's thinking. He realized the Lord was his triumph, that God was fighting his battles, and it caused him to shout, "Lord, how majestic is Your name!" Verses one and nine, which bookend this psalm, are more than praise. They are a statement of faith. "O Lord, our Lord, how majestic is your name in all the earth! You have set your glory above the heavens . . . O Lord, our Lord, how majestic is your name in all the earth!"

Let's focus on the sentence, "You have set your glory above the heavens." What could be above the heavens? David seemed to be saying that you could go past the end of the universe, beyond the realm of creation, and still you wouldn't begin to touch God's glory. That's a challenge to our minds, which are wrapped up in a finite understanding of all things. We understand distance, for example, through tangible things, points that can be measured. By contrast, God not only stands above created existence, but He creates existence. He is outside of it. With this perspective, we see we don't have the capacity to understand His existence in totality. He exists beyond all knowledge, wisdom, and reason. We'll never arrive at a satisfactory concept of God by exploring the extent of His power in a created thing. His power is of a completely different kind, His existence radically other than anything we can know.

So here in Psalm 8 we see David leaping out of his skin, his mind blown by the huge reality of God's infinite nature. David was saying that

ecause God's glory is far above any knowledge we might have of the
eavens, He is to be honored and revered in everything concerning our
ves. The Lord is omnipotent, yet He is also omnipresent, everywhere at
ll times. Therefore, the majestic God over all creation is also with you in
our room as you cry in the night. He doesn't have to rend the heavens to
ome to your side because He is already with you.

One phrase in Psalm 8 can be seen as a play on words from a previous
salm, and it is used to powerful effect. "You have set your glory above
he heavens" (Psalm 8:1). We have seen the word "set" before, in Psalm 2 as
David described kings and rulers setting themselves in rebellion against
God. The rulers of the world are set in their rebellion while God is set in
His glory; which do you think will win out? According to David, the victor
obviously is the Lord. He triumphs over all His enemies. God's glory does
not fluctuate. There isn't more or less of it at different times. His glory is
immeasurable, and it is also undefeatable.

Next, in the space of one verse, David moved from describing God's
power as heavenly and majestic to invoking an image of the lowest, most
helpless state possible. "Out of the mouth of babies and infants, you have
established strength" (Psalm 8:2). There couldn't be a greater distance
between these two points, from the highest reaches of the cosmos to
he lowest cry of a baby. What did David intend with this verse? How,
exactly, do babies and infants establish God's strength? The rest of the
verse adds some insight. "Out of the mouth of babies and infants, you
have established strength because of your foes, to still the enemy and
he avenger" (Psalm 8:2). This earthy verse seems like a totally separate
sermon from the first verse, which extols God's awesome majesty. Don't
be fooled, because this is not a change of subject. The opening two verses
of Psalm 8 are intricately related.

Let's start by focusing on the three things mentioned at the end of verse two: foes, enemies, and avengers. God is basically in a battle with the rulers of nations. We already know from Psalm 2 that nations rage against Lord, rising up against Him and His Son. Meanwhile, the psalmist asked, "Lord, I'm surrounded by enemies and need to be rescued. I plead with You, please, come and defeat them!"

I believe that in Psalm 8 David had a revelation, and it brought forth high praise from his heart and mouth. His revelation was, "Lord, these are Your battles, not mine. The fight belongs to You. I have peace." Nothing is as helpless as a baby, and yet its cries can call down the greatest power in existence.

What is causing anxiety for you? What are you wrestling with? What worries are stressing you? They aren't your battles. Lay them all down. Bring them to Jesus, casting your cares on Him, for He cares for you. Tell Him, "Lord, these are Your enemies, and You triumph over them." Your current enemy may be a disease, financial pressures, marital stress, or strained relationships. You can't conquer them in your own wisdom and strength. You have to trust the direction and power of the Holy Spirit to deal with them.

In his new frame of mind, one of ecstatic praises for God, David wasn't in denial that he had foes. How do we conduct spiritual warfare if there isn't an enemy? What soldier goes to battle believing he has no opponent? That wasn't David's thinking. His mental shift had to do with God's protection and undefeatable nature. In this psalm, David was more conscious of God's history of victories and deliverances than he was of his own trials. Before this, David thought of his enemies as high and his faith as low. Then, in a sudden turn, his faith was high and his enemies were low, easily defeated by the Lord. Often, the right weapon for our warfare is simply a correct nderstanding of Who God is. That's what makes the simplest cry of a babe powerful statement of faith that can reduce our enemies to nothing.

Psalm 8 reveals that God uses small things to bring down enemies. f you or I were going into battle against a fierce enemy, we naturally ould want to arm ourselves with the vastest military possible along ith massive weapons. This psalm, however, shows us that God emonstrates His strength through things the world sees as small, weak nd insignificant.

You may have heard a famous story from church history in which child spoke a word that confounded the ruling religious leaders. The tory is found in *Foxe's Book of Martyrs*. Centuries ago, a faithful Scottish astor preached powerfully prophetic sermons that offended the church nd society, and he was sentenced to be burned at the stake. As he was ed to his death, someone in the crowd shouted that he was a heretic vho preached the devil's word. Suddenly, the voice of a child rose from he throng crying, "He is not of the devil, because his words could not e spoken by the devil." The mob fell silent, confronted with the truth. Their false accusations were exposed by simple words from the mouth of a babe. The condemned pastor took courage as he faced death. God's power and glory were declared by someone the world deems small and insignificant, and it silenced those in opposition to the kingdom.

Something similar happened upon Jesus' triumphal entry into Jerusalem. When He arrived, He cleansed the temple of moneychangers and began healing the lame and blind. This probably rocked the world of the religious rulers, but the last straw for them was hearing young children shout Jesus' praises. "But when the chief priests and the scribes saw the wonderful things that he did, and the children crying out in the temple, 'Hosanna to the Son of David!' they were indignant, and they said to him, 'Do you hear what these are saying?'" (Matthew 21:15-16). Christ responded with truth from Psalm 8. "And Jesus said to them, 'Yes; have you never read, 'Out of the mouth of infants and nursing babies you have prepared praise'?" (Matthew 21:16).

Make no mistake, Jesus' actions with the moneychangers were a violent intervention. "... he overturned the tables of the money-changers and the seats of those who sold pigeons. He said to them, 'It is written "My house shall be called a house of prayer," but you make it a den of robbers'" (Matthew 21:12-13). This startling scene shows God bringing His righteousness to bear on impurity. The scene is more than that, however. Restoring God's temple to a house of prayer wasn't only a matter of purity but of justice. The blind and lame had been neglected by the temple leaders while the moneychangers were given space to do business. Jesus' actions were about restoring the temple as place of mercy and healing.

One would think the chief priest and scribes would be overjoyed at the wonderful things they saw Jesus doing. Instead, they were indignant. Maybe they were bewildered, unable to comprehend such works. Regardless, they were offended at hearing the children's praises for Jesus, "Look at the amazing things happening in the temple! Only God could do this. The Lord is surely among us!"

Such praise enrages Satan, because it tears down the enemy's strength. Praise sets things in their right order, readjusting our vision to God's majesty. It also shines a holy light on darkness, exposing it as ultimately weak and proclaiming God as victor who triumphs over all opposition.

Nature itself contains the most profound lessons on how God uses small things to reveal His power. When U.S. scientists engineered the first atomic explosion, they immediately began plotting for a greater one, a 10,000-megaton blast. It would be 670,000 times more powerful than ιe bomb dropped on Hiroshima. That kind of power is unfathomable to s, yet it is revealed to us in a single atom. A split atom can ignite a chain eaction with the explosive power to wipe out not just cities but nations. Iow think of the vast number of atoms in the universe. It is estimated hat they number ten quadrillion vigintillions, or one times ten to the ixty-third power. That's a lot of zeros. The confounding fact remains hat if you were to split a single microscopic atom, it would wipe out a nassive portion of the human race.

While Psalm 8 tells us how God demonstrates His power through small hings that are seemingly insignificant, His power exceeds the largest set of zeros we could ever conceive. The fact is 10 quadrillion vigintillions is a inite number, but God's power is infinite, as is His love for us.

David had a personal grasp of how God demonstrated His power hrough small things. He was just a boy when God told the prophet Samuel o anoint him as Israel's future king. David brought glory to the Lord when ιe stepped onto the field of battle and slew the supposedly undefeatable ;iant Goliath. Likewise, God used the stuttering Moses to deliver a tiny nation of abused slaves from the powerful clutches of one of the world's nightiest nations. Such examples of the humble confounding the wise are ictually common throughout Scripture.

In the New Testament, the apostle Paul said something similar when ιe wrote, "But [the Lord] said to me, 'My grace is sufficient for you, for my power is made perfect in weakness.' Therefore I will boast all the more gladly of my weaknesses, so that the power of Christ may rest upon me" (2 Corinthians 12:9). Paul's statement here is completely countercultural but also counterintuitive. When you feel incapable or unable, you think you're not useful for anything, the truth is you're in exactly the right position for God to use you. Through your weakness, He may demonstrate His power over obstacles that are insurmountable to us. He does this not only to bless us but also to bring hope to others facing their own difficulties.

David marveled at the wonder of God's powerful love and care for creatures as insignificant as human beings. "When I look at your heavens, the work of your fingers, the moon and the stars, which you have set in place, what is man that you are mindful of him, and the son of man that you care for him?" (Psalm 8:3). David obviously didn't have access to the scientific knowledge we have today thanks to things like the Hubble Telescope. We're told there are an estimated 500 billion galaxies and 320 sextillion stars and that the universe spans 93 billion light years in distance. These kinds of mind-blowing facts can make us feel small and insignificant, but David had an insight about our significance that is equally mind-blowing. Modern science has come to prove it.

In terms of proportion, the distance between my six-foot body and the farthest reaches of the universe—a distance of ninety-three billion light years—is the same distance between my six-foot body and the smallest atom inside my body. This means humankind sits at the very center of all we know to exist. We're neither as low as the smallest things nor as high as the biggest things. That is what David pondered. "We're below the angels and yet we are crowned with Your glory, Lord. Though we are weak and small, You have called us to have dominion over everything." David often used figurative speech to describe God in physical terms so that we might better relate to the heavenly Father. He did this in Psalm 8, mentioning "the work of your fingers, the moon and the stars, which you have set in place" (Psalm 8:3). By using fingers in his imagery, David implied, "If God accomplished such magnificent work with His mere fingers, imagine what He could do with His mighty arm. The very smallest part of God is sufficient for our greatest needs."

Psalm 8 includes yet another reference found throughout the New Testament. "You have given him dominion over the works of your hands; you have put all things under his feet" (Psalm 8:6). This reference is to Adam in Genesis, when the Lord gave him dominion over the earth and everything in it. Paul invoked this when he wrote, " . . . in fact Christ has been raised from the dead, the first fruits of those who have fallen asleep. For as by a man came death, by a man has come also the resurrection of the dead. For as in Adam all die, so also in Christ shall all be made alive" (1 Corinthians 15:20-22). As you know, Adam's dominion was subverted by Satan's deception, and the fall affected us all. "And you were dead in the trespasses and sins in which you once walked, following the course of this world, following the prince of the power of the air, the spirit that is now at work in the sons of disobedience—among whom we all once lived in the passions of our flesh, carrying out the desires of the body and the mind, and were by nature children of wrath, like the rest of mankind" (Ephesians 2:1-3).

The dominion that was meant for Adam was restored at the cross through God's righteousness. Paul assures us that all things are beneath Christ's feet, fully under His dominion, and the Lord is at work crushing the enemy who came to steal, kill, and destroy. "The God of peace will soon crush Satan under your feet" (Romans 16:20). Christ has given us back the inheritance that Satan tried to rob. His righteousness has positioned us with power and authority over the realms of darkness both in our lives and in society. By His authority, we have a role in the work of His kingdom. . . . because of the great love with which he loved us, even when we were dead in our trespasses, made us alive together with Christ—by grace you have been saved—and raised us up with him and seated us with him in the heavenly places in Christ Jesus" (Ephesians 2:4-6).

Paul summed up the extensive nature of God's dominion and it power for our lives. " . . . having the eyes of your hearts enlightened that you may know what is the hope to which he has called you, what are the riches of his glorious inheritance in the saints, and what is the immeasurable greatness of his power toward us who believe, according to the working of his great might that he worked in Christ when he raised him from the dead and seated him at his right hand in the heavenly places, far above all rule and authority and power and dominion, and above every name that is named, not only in this age but also in the one to come. And he put all things under his feet and gave him as head over all things to the church, which is his body, the fullness of him who fills all in all" (Ephesians 1:18-23). In this glorious passage, Paul drove home the truth that everything is under Christ's feet. He is head over all, and as His body, we are to enact His kingdom work with power.

Finally, the author of Hebrews also quoted Psalm 8 in a passage encompassing everything we've talked about in this chapter. "For it was not to angels that God subjected the world to come, of which we are speaking It has been testified somewhere, 'What is man, that you are mindful of him, or the son of man, that you care for him? You made him for a little while lower than the angels; you have crowned him with glory and honor putting everything in subjection under his feet.' Now in putting everything in subjection to him, he left nothing outside his control. At present, we do not yet see everything in subjection to him. But we see him who for a little while was made lower than the angels, namely Jesus, crowned with glory and honor because of the suffering of death, so that by the grace of God he might taste death for everyone. For it was fitting that he, for whom and by whom all things exist, in bringing many sons to glory, should make the founder of their salvation perfect through suffering" (Hebrews 2:5-10).

Clearly, Psalm 8 contains truths so central to our faith that writer after writer in Scripture refers to it. I remind you of this amazing statement from the passage in Hebrews 2:8, "He left nothing outside his control." Do we really believe this truth when we're in the trial of our lives? Or do we believe God has looked away and abandoned us to battle our enemies alone? David told us emphatically that God knows what He's doing. The Lord knows the enemy's plans as well as the exact time He is going to defeat those plans. We can be sure He uses every event of our lives for His greater glory, and He uses small things to accomplish it.

Through a small wooden cross on a small hill called Golgotha, every principality and power of darkness in the universe was defeated. Through a small crown of thorns placed cruelly on His head, Jesus suffered and bore the weight of all sins of all humanity throughout all of time. Through the mouths of infants and babes, the greatest power of all is proclaimed and exalted.

Like David, at times you have asked, "Where can I find hope? Where is the cure for my anxiety, stress, doubt, fear, selfishness, and lust? What is my remedy? God doesn't seem to care. Am I on my own to battle all these enemies?" Your answer is in the mouths of babes: Jesus reigns over all things. He laid down His life for you. His resurrection from a small grave, witnessed by insignificant people, is the power of the Gospel. His good news has you fully in its grasp. Therefore, you can say, "I have been crucified with Christ. It is no longer I who live, but Christ who lives in me. And the life I now live in the flesh I live by faith in the Son of God, who loved me and gave himself for me" (Galatians 2:20).

This, ultimately, is the reason for David's praise in Psalm 8. In our small lives amid a vast universe, our majestic God has made us agents of His glory.

CHAPTER TEN

Psalm 9

When Our "How Long, O Lord" Is Finally Over

To the choirmaster: according to Muth-labben.

A Psalm of David.

1 I will give thanks to the Lord with my whole heart;

I will recount all of your wonderful deeds.

2 I will be glad and exult in you;

I will sing praise to your name, O Most High.

3 When my enemies turn back,

they stumble and perish before your presence.

4 For you have maintained my just cause;

you have sat on the throne, giving righteous judgment.

5 You have rebuked the nations; you have made the wicked perish;

you have blotted out their name forever and ever.

6 The enemy came to an end in everlasting ruins;

their cities you rooted out;

the very memory of them has perished.

7 But the Lord sits enthroned forever;

he has established his throne for justice,

8 and he judges the world with righteousness;

he judges the peoples with uprightness.

9 The Lord is a stronghold for the oppressed,

   a stronghold in times of trouble.

10 And those who know your name put their trust in you,

   for you, O Lord, have not forsaken those who seek you.

11 Sing praises to the Lord, who sits enthroned in Zion!

   Tell among the peoples his deeds!

12 For he who avenges blood is mindful of them;

   he does not forget the cry of the afflicted.

13 Be gracious to me, O Lord!

   See my affliction from those who hate me,

   O you who lift me up from the gates of death,

14 that I may recount all your praises,

   that in the gates of the daughter of Zion

   I may rejoice in your salvation.

15 The nations have sunk in the pit that they made;

   in the net that they hid, their own foot has been caught.

16 The Lord has made himself known; he has executed judgment;

   the wicked are snared in the work of their own hands. Higgaion. Selah

17 The wicked shall return to Sheol,

   all the nations that forget God.

18 For the needy shall not always be forgotten,

   and the hope of the poor shall not perish forever.

19 Arise, O Lord! Let not man prevail;

   let the nations be judged before you!

20 Put them in fear, O Lord!

   Let the nations know that they are but men! Selah

HROUGH THE FIRST SEVEN PSALMS, David cried out a question that
ach of us can relate to, if we've lived long enough. Lamenting his many
rials, he constantly asked, "How long, O Lord?" Night after night, deep in
nguish, he wept so hard that tears soaked his pillow. Day after day, he cried,
;od, how long will I suffer these pains in my body? How long will my son
e against me? Have my sins ruined my life?"

You may have uttered David-like cries in any of your situations. Finally,
our breakthrough happened. You entered a new season, no longer needing
o ask in agony, "How long?" That was David's situation when he wrote
'salm 9. In the preceding chapters, we saw that David had to flee his son
bsalom, who led a revolt against his father, taking away David's throne.
le lived on the run, hiding in caves and among rocks. He suffered not
mly great loss but also deep heartaches and torment of soul. He was falsely
ccused of treason by the family of his predecessor, Saul. At the same time,
le lived under genuine guilt and shame after the public exposure of his
cts of adultery and murder.

Many reading this can relate to some of David's anguish. We wonder
f God hears us when we cry, "Lord, will my child ever speak to me again?
low long will I have to watch bills pile up as I live paycheck to paycheck?
Vill my marriage ever be restored? God, is there any hope for me at all?"
Ve get weary of praying desperately to make our deepest needs known
o the Lord. At times, our prayers are agony, yet every such lament is a
ry of hope. When you're spilling to God from your gut, even angrily or
accusingly, it reveals that you have hope.

The philosopher Friedrich Nietzsche didn't like the hope that
Christianity offered. He called it abusive. He observed Christians praying
about their problems and crises, seeking God to answer their unmet needs,
and he scoffed. He saw people hanging onto hope when he thought they

should abandon all hope. He concluded, "Hope in reality is the worst of all evils because it prolongs the torments of man." You might be familiar with the famous verse from Proverbs regarding hope. "Hope deferred makes the heart sick" (Proverbs 13:12). When hope doesn't seem worth holding onto, our hearts grow sick with despair. The answer isn't to abandon hope, however, but rather to find healing for our hearts in order to maintain our hope.

God does two things with our hope. One way God responds to our hope is to meet the outer need over which we are seeking Him. His other response has to do with our inner need, our heart's condition. Oftentimes He works on our heart while orchestrating a path to resolve our outer situation. This keeps us from becoming heartsick as we await deliverance. In short, we need two deliverances from God: one that strengthens our hope and one that delivers us from our trial.

Most of us don't realize how important hope is in our daily struggles. Once hope is abandoned, we start to despair, becoming despondent and angry and wanting to reject God. The Lord doesn't cast us out over any of these feelings. On the contrary, His nature is to heal the brokenhearted. He doesn't turn His back on the wounded or the discouraged but instead repairs our brokenness. We may think He doesn't want to hear our anger or despondency, but He actually invites and encourages our cries. God already knows what's in our hearts, so it's important for us to express those things to Him. We may be tempted with thoughts of "I've lost hope. I'm on my last leg of believing God," and He wants us to bring that admission to Him.

We tend to deal with hope in one of two ways in the midst of hard trials. The first way is to diminish our hope. We simply don't hope for too much. We minimize our expectations, believing not for great things but for just enough to survive and pass through life adequately. We fear asking the Lord for too much. Like any good father, however, God loves to give

His children and wants us to ask Him for good things. That includes
ur requests for healing, deliverance, reconciliation, and restoration when
'e're suffering. If we diminish our hope, that can have side effects we
on't anticipate. By repressing one emotion, we reduce others at the same
me. We can't suppress hope without repressing joy, peace, and confidence
s well. Suppressing hope and longings may provide a temporary taste
f stability, but it shuts down any possibility of a genuine breakthrough.
Moreover, it doesn't involve faith.

A second way we deal with hope deferred is by becoming cynical. We
ome to where we no longer believe God for anything, much less for great
hings. We settle into a mindset of "God doesn't listen or answer. That's
he way it is and always will be. My marriage has always been broken and
von't ever change. Look at how many marriages end in divorce. Also, I
lon't think my child will ever break free of their addiction. Look at how
nany people have died using substances. The only breakthroughs I can
ver expect to happen for me or my loved ones will be in heaven."

The problem with this thinking is that you allow other people's
problems to dictate what your hope should be. God's reality for your life
sn't based on others' experiences but on your relationship with Him.

Hope becomes hard for people for yet another reason. They get
hurt because what they hope for doesn't come to pass. The truth is God
doesn't promise to fulfill everything we hope will come to pass. Once we
diminish hope, though, becoming a cynic, we stop hoping for anything.
This guarantees that nothing will come to pass for us; or if it does, we'll
have no joy in it.

I realize I have had thousands of breakthroughs in my life. Ask yourself
honestly if the same has been true for you. I'm in my sixties now, and over
he passing years, I have cried out to God many times, "How long, O Lord?"

Though I have enjoyed many breakthroughs, there is always another crisis to face. It's simply a fact that we may never escape troubles, trial heartaches and pain that drive us to cry, "Lord, when will You answer me? In those times, it's easy to forget the multitude of breakthroughs God ha provided us. As I've grown older, I've remembered more often to thank God for everything He's brought me through. Having gratitude doesn' mean we shouldn't allow our hearts to grieve. The opposite is true. David' many lamenting psalms demonstrate that God wants us to bring our every grief to Him.

Think of David's life. This man of great faith saw extraordinary things take place as he responded to the Lord. He slew lions, bears and a giant enemy soldier. He became king over a nation and brought down the mighty Philistine army. Crowds sang his praises for his incredible military victories. He had the amazing son Solomon who did brilliant works of a different kind. Through all of his wonderful blessings, David wrote songs of deep lament. That is a picture of life for, us too. God wanted David's honest cry, and the Lord encourages the same from us.

Even if we have experienced a thousand breakthroughs, we need not fear lamenting our present trial and calling on God for deliverance. In fact, our lament and our gratitude go hand in hand. Even at our lowest points of grief, we're able to say, "God, You have delivered me in the past You can do it again."

In Psalm 9, we see that a change has taken place in David's attitude At that point in David's life, his laments had been turned into a song of deliverance. In the line above this psalm, a telling phrase appears: "Muth labben," suggesting the song be sung with a certain familiar tune. Its melody was already known to Israelites, and David adapted different lyrics to fit it The meaning of the phrase is uncertain, but one way of reading it is that he original tune for the song was for the death of a son. David changed the lyrics to supply a new message to the song.

Decades ago, the musician Eric Clapton wrote a song about his toddler son who had died in a tragic accident. People were touched by Clapton's song "Tears in Heaven," and it sold millions all over the world. If "Muthlabben" does indeed refer to a song for the death of one's son, then it was as if David were saying, "You know that Eric Clapton song? For this occasion, let's change the title to 'Joy in Heaven.' We'll take the same tune of lament and sing it with new lyrics of praise."

That is the thrust of Psalm 9, and it is profound. In fact, this is what God wants to do in your life and in mine. He was saying, "I want you to take all your songs of lament, sorrow, pain, and loss and change the words as a new song rises up in you. The new song I'm giving you is one of victory. The new lyrics represent a new season in your life, a breakthrough I am leading you into."

As David moved out of a season of asking, "How long, O Lord?," he moved into a season of answered prayer. In Psalm 9, he was saying, "The Lord has set me free, giving me victory! I no longer mourn or cry myself to sleep. He has supplied my breakthrough, and I won't look back anymore. I am singing a new song."

If you start singing a new song without first lamenting, you might not believe wholeheartedly what you're singing. With God, we each have the ability to say anything at any time to express our hearts before Him. "Lord, here's what my marriage is like, and it's breaking my heart." "Here's what it's like to have a child who has turned from their faith." "Here's what it's like to fail at my dream job." I encourage you to sing your song of brokenheartedness to the Lord, openly and passionately, but sing it with hope, not cynicism. Sing it with the belief, "One day, I'll be singing this same tune but with different lyrics." Even Jesus prayed, "Let this cup pass from me" a cry that His soul was overwhelmed almost to the point of death. It was a prayer of lament; but later, on the other side of the cross, He declared "All power and authority have been given to me by the Father." This was a powerful new song, but to sing it, Jesus had to go through the cross.

For us, sometimes the hardships we go through are meant to build character, perseverance and faith. Psalm 9 reflected this in its powerful opening. David wrote, "I will give thanks to the LORD with my whole heart" (Psalm 9:1). For readers familiar with the preceding psalms, this wasn't just a declaration but a life statement. David was saying, "Something has changed in my life." He testified to this by enumerating all that God did for him. "I will recount all of your wonderful deeds. I will be glad and exult in you; I will sing praise to your name, O Most High" (Psalm 9:1-2). David's crises were behind him thanks to God's "wonderful deeds." His response to God's wonderful deliverance was "Lord, You've solved my problem and met my need. You have overcome all my crises. I will be glad and exult in You." So David recounted the amazing ways God accomplished his deliverance while he was powerless on his own. "When my enemies turn back, they stumble and perish before your presence" (Psalm 9:3). The Lord had fought his battles, and because of that, David knew his enemies weren't coming back. Whatever God brings down, He destroys completely.

In my years of ministry, I have worked with a lot of young men who battle addictions. They would come to me, saying, "I've had a breakthrough. My struggle is behind me!" Later, they would return to their addiction in a sad cycle. David was testifying here, "God's deliverance is not an up-and-down thing. My battle is resolved. My enemies have turned back and left me. They don't existent in my life anymore. I no longer have to face these struggles, because God made them perish." " . . . they stumble and perish before your presence" (Psalm 9:3). One version translates this as "because of your presence." The Lord's presence is the difference, no matter what your situation. Your breakthrough may be for a boss to recognize the unrewarded work you do. It may be for wisdom through a relational trial. It may be for much-needed life direction from an elder in the faith. These are all pressing realities, and maybe your hope for them has been deferred. The bottom line is that the negative things perish because of God's presence. The Lord enters your situation and shines a light on the darkness. Where death has existed, life enters through the glory of God's presence. He turns everything upside down for the good.

At this point in the psalm, David changed his focus from "I" to "you." His thoughts turned to God most high, Who has authority over all things. . . . you have sat on the throne, giving righteous judgment. You have rebuked the nations; you have made the wicked perish; you have blotted out their name forever and ever" (Psalm 9:4-5). God's righteous presence changed David's song. The Lord was healing brokenness and meeting needs, and David realized all that the Lord was doing for him. He declared, You changed this; You healed that; You rebuked my enemies and chased them all away. Lord, You are the victor, the conqueror and the king. You are the lover of my soul, the One Who meets all my needs according to Your riches in glory."

The deliverance was glorious, yet it came after a long time after David began crying, "How long, O Lord?" The message of Psalm 9 is God's solid promise to you of a new song. It might not happen this week or this year or perhaps a longer time, but it will happen. Let hope arise in your heart because the enemy that has plagued you will come to an everlasting ruin. God has cut it down at the roots. "The enemy came to an end in everlasting ruins; their cities you rooted out; the very memory of them has perished"

(Psalm 9:6). Note that last phrase. Not only has God caused your enemy to perish, but at some point you won't even remember that it existed in your life. "But the Lord sits enthroned forever; he has established his throne for justice" (Psalm 9:7). From His throne, God is working His justice, and part of that is to bring an end to our enemies. We may not sense God's just-ness when we're in the midst of our trial, continually crying, "How long, O God?" We may even begin to accuse Him, "Why have You abandoned me? Why won't You hear my prayer?" Psalm 9 demonstrates how God has planned a perfectly timed moment to come into your situation and shine His light. When that moment comes, we realize, "Lord, I'm sorry I ever accused You. I never should have thought of You as being anything but upright."

God understands our lament. That's because even in our sorrowful song, we express faith. "Lord, my soul is breaking inside, but I cry to You because I know my soul is heard. My spirit is so far down I can't summon even a syllable of praise. Despite the darkness all around me and my enemies attacking, though, I know You are good." "The Lord is a stronghold for the oppressed, a stronghold in times of trouble" (Psalm 9:9). Every lament is a marriage of pain and hope, and David expressed something very important for us. While we wait and cry, "How long?," the Lord's presence is with us all the way through the moment He changes our circumstances. God is a stronghold for us through our long times of trouble, and all that time He is at work changing our heart as well.

"And those who know your name put their trust in you, for you, O Lord, have not forsaken those who seek you" (Psalm 9:10). What does it mean to know His name? It means experiencing His loving grace and transforming power. Through that experience, it becomes possible for us to know His goodness and to place our trust in Him. Knowing God's name isn't just an intellectual exercise or a theological study. It is highly personal.

To whom do we sing our new song? "Sing praises to the Lord, who
sits enthroned in Zion! Tell among the peoples his deeds!" (Psalm 9:11).
Our new song is both worship we offer to the Lord and a testimony of
God's goodness we offer to the world. We not only "exult" in the Lord. We
also tell people, "Here's what my life was like, and God did this to turn
around for me." Our testimony actually contains the names of God:
victor, savior, protector and healer. That brings hope to people. As we
sing His praises from our own experience, we're ministering to others. A
core part of this testimony is that God hears our cries and doesn't forget
us in our affliction. "For he who avenges blood is mindful of them; he
does not forget the cry of the afflicted. Be gracious to me, O Lord! See
my affliction from those who hate me, O you who lift me up from the
gates of death" (Psalm 9:12-13). David didn't say, "God, please, lift me from
the gates of death," as he did in previous psalms. Rather, he testified,
"You are the one who lifts me up from the gates of death." His focus had
shifted from his need to his God. David could only make this shift if his
confidence was renewed. His song had become one of courage, strength
and faith because he recounted all the ways that God had been faithful
to him. David's words in Psalm 9 were full of new life. His deferred hope
had finally been resurrected as he saw deliverance, and the impact was
dramatic. As the Proverb goes, "Hope deferred makes the heart sick, but a
desire fulfilled is a tree of life" (Proverbs 13:12).

   At this point, David refocused his attention once more to things on
a grander scale. He shifted gears once more in this psalm, writing, "The
nations have sunk in the pit that they made; in the net that they hid, their
own foot has been caught" (Psalm 9:15). He moved his attention from an
individual lament to grief on a national scale. In this verse, he cried out
for his nation and its leaders not to forget God. May we all pray for this

in the United States. The need for a spiritual breakthrough in our country is obvious. We need to see God's delivering power break the enemy's grip over laws and institutions, from schools to government to politics. All of these have sunk into a pit of their own making and are snared. "The wicked shall return to Sheol, all the nations that forget God" (Psalm 9:17). As we pray, let us all seek a new song not just for our lives and families but also for our country. May God forgive us, cleanse us and renew us.

David was still speaking of nations as he continued, "For the needy shall not always be forgotten, and the hope of the poor shall not perish forever" (Psalm 9:18). When God moves, the poor and needy renew their hope because the Lord has them in mind, stirring His church to act on their behalf. The Lord invites us to cry as David cried, "Arise, O Lord! Let no man prevail; let the nations be judged before you! Put them in fear, O Lord! Let the nations know that they are but men! Selah" (Psalm 9:19-20). Humans have some power, but God has all power. So in our affliction, whether individual or national, let us seek Him to rise up and judge according to His righteousness and justice. No concern is too small for Him, and no issue is too big. He can change hearts or nations with equal power.

As you await your new song amid your suffering, hold onto hope. Trust Jesus both for your problems and for the nation, because He is faithful. Seek His healing for your heart sickness, and marry your song of lament to hope. We are only men and women, but He is Lord, ruler over all.

CHAPTER ELEVEN

Psalm 10
Is God Absent?

1 Why, O Lord, do you stand far away?

    Why do you hide yourself in times of trouble?

2 In arrogance the wicked hotly pursue the poor;

    let them be caught in the schemes that they have devised.

3 For the wicked boasts of the desires of his soul,

    and the one greedy for gain curses and renounces the Lord.

4 In the pride of his face the wicked does not seek him;

    all his thoughts are, "There is no God."

5 His ways prosper at all times;

    your judgments are on high, out of his sight;

    as for all his foes, he puffs at them.

6 He says in his heart, "I shall not be moved;

    throughout all generations I shall not meet adversity."

7 His mouth is filled with cursing and deceit and oppression;

    under his tongue are mischief and iniquity.

8 He sits in ambush in the villages;

    in hiding places he murders the innocent.

His eyes stealthily watch for the helpless;

9   he lurks in ambush like a lion in his thicket;

he lurks that he may seize the poor;

    he seizes the poor when he draws him into his net.

10 The helpless are crushed, sink down,

and fall by his might.

11 He says in his heart, "God has forgotten,

he has hidden his face, he will never see it."

12 Arise, O Lord; O God, lift up your hand;

forget not the afflicted.

13 Why does the wicked renounce God

and say in his heart, "You will not call to account"?

14 But you do see, for you note mischief and vexation,

that you may take it into your hands;

to you the helpless commits himself;

you have been the helper of the fatherless.

15 Break the arm of the wicked and evildoer;

call his wickedness to account till you find none.

16 The Lord is king forever and ever;

the nations perish from his land.

17 O Lord, you hear the desire of the afflicted;

you will strengthen their heart; you will incline your ear

18 to do justice to the fatherless and the oppressed,

so that man who is of the earth may strike terror no more.

WHERE IS GOD IN OUR time of need? If you've been a Christian for any length of time, you've surely considered this question. Where exactly is the Lord when our prayers go unanswered? Is He absent? Why does He seem distant from us during our trials? Where is He when our dreams go unfulfilled, dreams that are based on His promises, promises that we expected Him to keep? In some seasons of trial, we're assaulted by terrors fearing we'll never emerge from our struggle and that maybe God has

andoned us. I've been there, and I can tell you that Psalm 10 has power to
ark a profound shift in your life.

In the first nine psalms, David posed many questions to God. In doing
, he set a precedent for us in seeking the Lord honestly and openly so
at we may fully trust Him. David experienced so many trials that a
uman can face, and his example shows how we can bring everything in
ur hearts to God, withholding nothing. In previous psalms, David asked,
ord, how long will You allow these troubles in my life?" Here in Psalm
, the psalmist asked a different question. "Why, O Lord, do you stand far
way? Why do you hide yourself in times of trouble?" (Psalm 10:1). David's
ry was like those of so many Christians I've known over decades. "Why
re You so distant from me while I go through these horrible things? Why
o You stand so far away from me as I suffer?"

In verses two through eleven, David described what made him
eel like God was distant. After his opening question, David began a
ompelling case for God's intervention. He pointed out, "In arrogance
he wicked hotly pursue the poor" (Psalm 10:2). The word for "poor" here
s associated with another word that appears in this psalm, "afflicted."
avid saw evildoers abusing vulnerable people with an arrogance toward
iod. "For the wicked boasts of the desires of his soul, and the one greedy
or gain curses and renounces the Lord" (Psalm 10:3). Interestingly, David
ut forth two contrasting voices of desire in Psalm 10. First, there was the
oice of the boasting wicked, then there was the desire of the afflicted.
he latter voice reflected the heavy realities that the assaults of the
vicked brought upon them. "O Lord, you hear the desire of the afflicted"
Psalm 10:17). Psalm 10 is deeply emotional because it's so down to earth
n describing the pain involved in our struggles. In a sequence of several
erses, the weight of our troubles and their source become crystal clear.

When a forceful evildoer comes against us, the result can devastate us in ways we weren't prepared for. "The helpless are crushed, sink down, and fall by his might. He says in his heart, 'God has forgotten, he has hidden his face, he will never see it'" (Psalm 10:10-11). David knew this condition all too well. In Psalm 10, he turned it into a cry. "Arise, O Lord; O God, lift up your hand; forget not the afflicted" (Psalm 10:12). In other words, "Lord, don't forget me! Don't forget any of your afflicted people with our troubles piled on top of troubles." David then extolled God's awesome power to intervene for us. "But you do see, for you note mischief and vexation, that you may take it into your hands; to you the helpless commits himself; you have been the helper of the fatherless. Break the arm of the wicked and evildoer; call his wickedness to account till you find none" (Psalm 10:14-15).

Psalm 10's premise is that we all acknowledge the terrors, trials, and troubles that come our way. David's terrors led to a cry of truth in the final verse. " . . . you will incline your ear to do justice . . . so that man who is of the earth may strike terror no more" (Psalm 10:17-18). This was a cry of unmet need, giving voice to our anguish as we sense God's absence. The cry was, "God, let the evil workers of terror strike no more."

Our terrors can take the form of daily troubles. "God, You won't let the wicked work terror anymore. Let this marital strife be no more. Let my sickness strike no more. Let my financial crisis strike no more. Let all of these terrors strike me no longer, and stop those who commit them." In crying out, we acknowledge the reality of our terrors. However, there is also a Part B to this acknowledgment, and for many of us it is harder to bear. This is the acknowledgment of our unrealized desires, hopes that we trusted the Lord to fulfill based on His promises. When these longings go unfulfilled, He seems absent from the deepest part of our heart. I have had to face this personally at certain times in my life. I have also seen it in thers through my pastoral counseling over forty-plus years of ministry. The problems that people brought into my office weren't usually their real need. Their deeper need was to know that God heard them. They told me, "I pray and pray about this, and it seems like God doesn't hear me. I can't seem to reach Him. I'm in this terrifying situation and I don't know where He is." This supposed silence is frightening for anyone to experience. If God doesn't come through for us, where else can we turn? We have no other source of hope. As Peter said, "Lord, to whom shall we go? You have the words of eternal life" (John 6:68).

I have written many times of the crisis of my son's severe drug addiction. His prolonged struggle was an excruciating period of absolute terror for my wife and me. What if he overdosed? What if he committed a crime and was jailed? What if he ended up homeless, wandering the streets in a haze, vulnerable to muggings or worse? Each of these things actually happened to him. Each time, our terror grew greater. With every frightening incident, our dreams for our gifted, beautiful son to thrive in a life of following Jesus were hammered to dust. I remember praying, "God, are You hearing me? The more I pray for our son, the worse he gets. If I've ever needed You to stand with me, it is now in our pain and tears. I'm confused about You right now. Where are You?" Our trial over our son was so unrelenting that we wound up asking questions we never thought we would consider. "Are You really there, God? Is Your word really true? Your absence is fueling doubt. You seem to answer our easy, daily prayers, but in the hardest time of our lives You seem to be nowhere. We wonder if You even exist."

When it comes to asking deeply honest questions from the depths of our terrified souls, many of us opt out. We simply don't want to go there. We don't want to face that God may be failing us in our hardest trials and is bringing down our soul. Instead of facing the pain, we leap over it to declare, "Everything is fine." Often to obtain true confidence in God's Word though, our souls have to go into that deep valley. To gain the kind of trust God wants for us, we may be called to wrestle with His Word. Our most sincere prayer may sometimes be "Lord, I don't get this. Your Word doesn't line up with what's happening in my life. Nothing about this makes any sense." That is a prayer God honors. Instead, however, many of us repress our questions. Over time, our beaten-down soul can become a boiling cauldron of confusion. We end up turning all of this on ourselves, thinking "I can't go to God with my anger and frustration. He'll decimate me."

No, God already knows what's inside us. He knows every question we hide and every emotion we repress. He wants us to bring it all out of the hiding place we've created and into His presence. Again and again David cried out to God, "Lord, please, hear my groaning. Attend to my cries." If we don't get all of our woundedness out, we'll keep stewing in it, and it will just keep building up within us. We know this from David's testimony in previous psalms. He spoke of having weak bones and a weary spirit. When he finally confessed his heart and made his plea to the Lord, new life sprang up in him. As we face our hard questions, it's important to understand we're dealing with two issues that are entwined. First is the worker of terror who afflicts us, and second is our desire for God to be present in our trial. The first issue is of a practical dimension while the second involves the spiritual realm.

When David described the evildoer who lies in wait to assault the vulnerable, he might easily have been describing Satan, who seeks to kill, steal, and destroy. "He sits in ambush in the villages; in hiding places he murders the innocent. His eyes stealthily watch for the helpless; he lurks in ambush like a lion in his thicket; he lurks that he may seize the poor; he seizes the poor when he draws him into his net. The helpless are crushed nk down, and fall by his might" (Psalm 10:8-9). In David's description, ye wicked one brought a horrible taunting that threatened real, physical onsequences yet also injected fear into the soul. We may hear similar taunts om the enemy: "Do you really think someone is going to do something yout this? There is no God Who will help you or stop me." "In the pride of is face the wicked does not seek him . . . He says in his heart, 'I shall not be yoved; throughout all generations I shall not meet adversity'" (Psalm 10:4-6).

In this part of the psalm, David remarked on his sense of God's iddenness in working his justice. "His (the evildoer's) ways prosper at ll times; your judgments are on high, out of his sight; as for all his foes, e puffs at them" (Psalm 10:5). The wicked assaults in your life may not ome from an obvious culprit. It could be the degrading voice of a spouse 'ho runs you down with verbal abuse. It could be the accusing tongue of a gossiper who spreads falsehoods about you. It could even be the voice f your child as they continually spout hatred toward you, causing you ɔ despair of ever having a healthy relationship with them. In every case, atan uses their hurtful words and lies to convince you you're worthless, loser, unworthy of God's grace and love. The harshest voice can actually e our own. I can't tell you the number of times I've left the podium fter preaching and thought, "I missed the correct point. The message vas unclear. There was no real content. This sermon was all driven by mbition. Nobody in the audience was helped by this." We begin to yelieve these voices, and God wants us freed from them. It's one thing to ye convicted of sin; we also have to be open to the voice of the Spirit for iealthy correction. God gives us discernment to know when the enemy s aiming fiery arrows at us. We have to stand on what Jesus says about is, not on lies that are meant to crush us. "The helpless are crushed, sink own, and fall by his might" (Psalm 10:10).

Psalm 10 contains four ways we are to quiet the lies that cause us to feel helpless. There are four steps to quieting Satan's lies. I call these the cry, the call, the commitment, and the confidence. With verse eighteen, David issued a cry for God "to do justice . . . so that man who is of the earth may strike terror no more" (Psalm 10:18).

Our first step is to cry out. We need not be afraid to pray, "Why, Lord?" This question may lead us into a valley where we give full voice to our disappointment. Ironically, this is a place we resist because we work so hard not to doubt God, and at times our prayers can sound as doubting as the disciple Thomas. "God, are You real or not? Are You present when I cry out to You?" David's cries assure me I can give voice to my own cries without fear. During my son's ordeal, my anguished cry led me into a deep valley where I faced a hard reality. I realized, "As I go through this, I have my wife's hand to hold. When she and I cry, we can hold each other. When one of us feels hopeless, we can hug the other. Lord, I don't have that with You. I don't feel connected to You. I feel closer to my wife than to You. I can pray and read Your Word, but I don't sense Your presence. I'm troubled and confused and I need something real from You. I don't have Your hand to hold."

After that valley experience, my son was delivered in a way that showed me God was at work all along. Our son fled his rehab problem and was running on the street when a concerned taxi driver saw him. As the cabby slowed his car, my son flagged him down. My son told him why he was running and asked to be taken to the airport. The cabby shook his head. He was a Christian and knew that my son needed rehab. "I'll drive you back there, at no charge," he said. Thankfully, my son listened and went with him.

The Lord intervened in our son's life this way nearly a dozen times. When he fled his problems headlong toward something worse, someone epped in miraculously to turn him around. Each instance was an answer

our prayers that terror would strike no more in our beloved son's life.

God's promises can be fulfilled in our lives by 1,000 people acting

His hands and feet. In answer to our desperate cry, His Spirit moves

rough people so that we never have to feel we're alone. When we grip a

elping human hand, we grip His. Through our experience with our son's

ddiction, I began to hear God answer me, "When you cry, I'll show you

y hands, face, and heart through a multitude of people I send across

our path." These people may be an unknown taxi driver, or they may be

friend who calls you on some lonely night saying, "I want you to know

m praying for you." After I wrestled with God in the valley, my eyes were

pened in new ways to His work in my life. Had I denied my problems or

st addressed them on the surface, never looking at the contents of my

eart, I wouldn't have dealt with the doubt that grew inside me. The Lord

rged me to express my unbelief to Him, and He answered by opening

y eyes to His merciful workings in a way I'd never seen. This led to a

ifferent cry, more like David's. "Arise, O Lord; O God, lift up your hand;

orget not the afflicted" (Psalm 10:12).

This is the second step in ridding ourselves of Satan's lies. It is when

e say, "I am no longer afraid to cry out in honesty to God. Now I will

all on Him, 'Lord, please, will You do this?'" It's a simple shift from a cry

f absolute terror to instead calling on God to move. It happens when we

elieve that He is present, hears us, understands our pain and takes up

ur cause. "But you do see, for you note mischief and vexation, that you

nay take it into your hands" (Psalm 10:14). Consider two brief words in

his verse: "you note." God is recording all that the wicked do to vex the

ulnerable. Knowing this, what does it do for your soul? God is not only

istening to your cry but is watching your enemy, because He is going to destroy their evil work. Simply put, judgment is coming. God is going to throw Satan into the pit forever, and your earthly enemy's works will be vanquished as well. The Lord will give you a new song to sing.

The third step is to commit ourselves to trust God to work in His way. This means committing every terror in our lives into His hands and trusting He will deliver us from every voice that crushes us. " . . . to you the helpless commits himself; you have been the helper of the fatherless" (Psalm 10:14).

The fourth and final step in ridding ourselves of terror is confidence. By crying, calling, and committing, we enter a glorious confidence that says, "I know my redeemer lives. He is not absent. I know He hears my cries. He has seen me when I've been helpless, stepped on, crushed, and fallen. Now, when people lie about me, or my spouse shouts obscenities at me, or my child spouts hatred at me, I don't absorb it. Instead, I call on the Lord. 'God, You've heard my cry. I ask You to have mercy. I commit all my troubles to You, and I am confident You will meet me."

There are two types of confidence in God. One kind of confidence is to believe the Lord's power to carry us through the storm or to take away the storm altogether. This is a trusting belief that He is capable of doing it. The second kind of confidence is to know that though the storm rages, God is watching and doing a supernatural work within us that will advance His kingdom. "O Lord, you hear the desire of the afflicted; you will strengthen their heart" (Psalm 10:17). This second kind of confidence is grounded in a knowledge that a day of redemption is coming, one of deliverance and recompense. This is the hope of every believer who lives with terror or wounds or has felt downcast and alone. Their hope is contained in the final verse of the psalm. " . . . so that man who is of the earth may strike terror no more" (Psalm 10:18).

God has taken note of what Satan and all workers of evil are doing, pinpointed it and placed it under His constant gaze, awaiting His time to judge and destroy it. The evil worker will no longer strike terror in you. Instead, you will scoff at him. You can stand in confidence knowing that his lies are false and that God will stop his assaults. You can do this because you will have seen that God is not absent at all but is present with you and will take action.

This entire cycle—to cry, call, commit, and have confidence—is demonstrated for us in the cross of Christ. He went through Good Friday, when He was mocked with a crown of thorns and His friends abandoned Him. He cried out as He was crucified, "Father, why have you forsaken me?" (Mark 15:34). He called on the Father, committed Himself into the Father's hands and was confident the Father would raise Him up. In this way, the cross not only redeems us from our terrors but shows us the path through terror to resurrection life. We must die to ourselves and be raised again with Christ. This death works something eternal in us, killing sin and confidence in the flesh yet also killing terrifying lies, nailing them to the cross. There is resurrection life on the other side of our valley, but we can't get there if we repress or deny our terrors. Resurrection life only comes after we pass through death.

Christ's very first sermon encapsulated all of this. "And as was his custom, he went to the synagogue on the Sabbath day, and he stood up to read. And the scroll of the prophet Isaiah was given to him. He unrolled the scroll and found the place where it was written, 'The Spirit of the Lord is upon me, because he has anointed me to proclaim good news to the poor. He has sent me to proclaim liberty to the captives and recovering of sight to the blind, to set at liberty those who are oppressed, to proclaim the year of the Lord's favor.' And he rolled up the scroll and gave it back to the attendant and sat down. And the eyes of all in th synagogue were fixed on him. And he began to say to them, 'Today thi scripture has been fulfilled in your hearing'" (Luke 4:17-21). This was a incredible proclamation. Jesus was quoting from Isaiah, and everyon in attendance was probably familiar with it. The rest of that passage i Isaiah predicted explicitly what Jesus would do for us in every generatio "... to proclaim the year of the Lord's favor, and the day of vengeanc of our God; to comfort all who mourn; to grant to those who mour in Zion—to give them a beautiful headdress instead of ashes, the oil o gladness instead of mourning, the garment of praise instead of a fain spirit; that they may be called oaks of righteousness, the planting of th Lord, that he may be glorified. They shall build up the ancient ruins; the shall raise up the former devastations; they shall repair the ruined citie the devastations of many generations" (Isaiah 61:2-4).

Here is a powerful vision of the kingdom of God. The Lord is going t bring down every work of evil, and His people will be His hands and fee to restore His way. Jesus was announcing, "I'm going to proclaim libert to captives, and they'll be liberated from fear and terror to do the work of the Father."

Jesus is faithful to bring this to pass in all of our lives. Our role i simple: to cry honestly before Him, to call on Him with every request, t commit all our fears to Him, and to stand confidently that He will rais us to new heights.

It is important to understand that our trials are never a one-time experience. Other crises will surely come, yet with each one there wil be a profound difference. We won't look at our battles as if God is usin them to punish us. Instead, with our history of going through valley we'll see our battles as training ground for warfare and we'll rejoice i

od's faithfulness to us. In whatever way He chooses to use these crises
our lives, He will bring us through as victors and not as victims.

Let out all your hurt out to Him. Don't repress it. Let Jesus take you
the place He wants you to go. Although the wicked act as though God
will not step in and bring justice, the psalmist knows otherwise. God
just allowing the wicked to ensnare himself and will eventually step
, and our prayer is that this happens swiftly. God will meet you in the
alley and will destroy every terror so that it strikes no more.

CHAPTER TWELVE

Psalm 11
In the Dark

1 In the Lord I take refuge;

how can you say to my soul,

"Flee like a bird to your mountain,

2 for behold, the wicked bend the bow;

they have fitted their arrow to the string

to shoot in the dark at the upright in heart;

3 if the foundations are destroyed,

what can the righteous do?"

4 The Lord is in his holy temple;

the Lord's throne is in heaven;

his eyes see, his eyelids test the children of man.

5 The Lord tests the righteous,

but his soul hates the wicked and the one who loves violence.

6 Let him rain coals on the wicked;

fire and sulfur and a scorching wind shall be the portion of their cup.

7 For the Lord is righteous;

he loves righteous deeds;

the upright shall behold his face.

THE TITLE OF THIS CHAPTER comes from verse two. " . . . for behold, th
wicked bend the bow; they have fitted their arrow to the string to shoot i
the dark at the upright in heart" (Psalm 11:2). Psalm 11 starts with a probler
and ends with a promise. In between, it addresses three questions we hav
about our times of troubling darkness and the assaults that come upon u
Our first question is "Where is God when we're in the dark?" The secon
is "How do we call on God when we're in the dark?" The third is "What i
God's commitment to us when we're in the dark?" When we are in nee
we seek the Lord's face for the light of His countenance to show us a wa
forward. He is our only reliable source when we're confused, drained, an
overwhelmed by the dark.

I once took classes from a respected professor of biblical counselin
who described his own years in the dark. My counseling professor's stor
was heartbreaking. As a child, he had been overweight, and his classmate
had ridiculed him mercilessly. The abuse went on for a long time anc
wounded him deeply. Maybe you can relate to some degree. Many o
us carry wounds from our childhood, a bully classmate, a father whc
abandoned the family, a mother who abused her children, or someone
else who traumatized us. If those experiences aren't dealt with and healec
the emotional scars from them follow us into adulthood.

David, the author of this psalm, knew he had a place to go in his
darkness. He opened by writing, "In the Lord I take refuge" (Psalm 11:1)
David was telling us we have hope of escape in our time of suffering and
difficulty, and that the Lord is the safe one to whom we can bring our cries
It is one thing to suffer through times of darkness when we bring it on
ourselves through a lifestyle of sinful behaviors. In that case, we expect
arrows to come. For the upright in heart, however, endlessly suffering
in the dark is troubling to the soul. For my counseling professor who

endured constant abuse and mockery as a child, deliverance had to come but seemed like it never would. This is the point where things get tough for people of faith. When our situation gets worse, when our pain increases and sufferings seem to multiply, we get confused. Our expectation is to see the light of God's face shining on us, but instead we remain helpless in the troubling dark. Moreover, as David said, the enemy fires arrows at us that we can't see coming.

In the case of my professor, things got frighteningly worse. His parents sent him to a summer camp where he suffered even worse abuse mentally, physically, and sexually. He spent an entire summer in torment and fear and was threatened with worse treatment if he told anyone about the abuse. Having nowhere to go with his boiling pain, it built up inside him. Later in his youth, his soul full of sorrow and outrage, he joined a gang. He sold drugs and committed others crimes that led to a prison sentence. It was a tragic culmination of a path that started in a darkness that was forced on him.

A beloved member of my family also suffered a long season of darkness that was forced on her. My maternal grandmother was a picture of kindness, the sort of person anyone would want as a grandparent. Sitting on her porch in a rocking chair, she sweetly awaited our arrival before starting her endless baking of cookies for us. My grandmother spent hours praying for her children and grandchildren. Many times, I walked into her living room to find her on her knees in prayer. Anyone looking from the outside would never guess that this lovely, holy woman was stuck in a dark season that never seemed to end. You see, my grandfather had a serious alcohol problem, and his drinking got to the point that he abused my grandmother terribly. He screamed at her, accused her of things she didn't do and struck her. My grandmother

stayed married to him, praying and hoping for a turnaround, but th
abuse and pain went on for decades. Finally, my grandfather came t
Christ and things changed. Through all the preceding years, though, m
grandmother never knew whether she would ever see a joyful day again

What do we do when we are endlessly shot with arrows in the dark
In the opening verse of Psalm 11, David answered what we do in long dar
seasons. "In the Lord I take refuge" (Psalm 11:1). He sought a haven of safet
in God. As we read in the previous psalm, David called out, "Lord, thes
trials never end. I have longings and desires to fulfill Your purposes i
my life, but those dreams seem to have died. When will You deliver me t
fulfill the things You have planned for me?"

Our need for relief in dark times is heightened as our troubles continu
As our pain intensifies and we don't feel God is responding, we migh
seek out another source. As a hurting teen, my professor turned to gan
life for a sense of belonging. That turned into crime and imprisonmen
For many of us, numbing our pain won't hold the same consequence bu
can take a toll nonetheless. Some seek relief in alcohol, porn, spending
overeating, sexual immorality or other supposed pleasures, anything tha
might distract from the unending pain. None of this works. In fact, it gives
us a false sense of fulfillment. As the fleeting pleasure dissipates, we're lef
not just empty but guilty. We have piled another type of anguish on top o
our pain, weighing down our soul; and the enemy's arrows become worse
The truth is that our longings can only be met in the Lord.

I love David's strong response to this crushing cycle. He said outright in
the opening verse, "In the Lord I take refuge." He was determined he would
look to no other source than God Himself. There, in the safe haven of the
Lord's presence, David understood he would continue to have dark times
So he cried to whoever was advising him, "How can you say to my soul

ee like a bird to your mountain'" (Psalm 11:1-2). David seemed to be saying, can't run away from my problems. How can I possibly escape to other iings?" David was resolute in trusting the Lord rather than fleeing. This ows us how it is possible for us to worship in the midst of our unending ark. Even in our worst moments, as my grandmother exemplified, it is ossible to worship if we run to the Lord's amazing refuge.

What can we do when it feels like our foundations are destroyed? avid addressed what it felt like to have solid ground removed from nderneath him. "If the foundations are destroyed, what can the ghteous do?" (Psalm 11:3). In asking the question, David knew that as ong as the foundations are in place, the upright have no need to fear.

Throughout the years, church leaders have used this verse to speak national and political concerns. They see foundations being destroyed s society holds up immoral aspects as good. Leaders are alarmed as they ee laws pass that oppose righteousness, diminish faith and that push he church aside. The context of this verse, however, makes clear that ts application is much more personal than political or national. David vas saying, "If the foundations of my life are threatened, if my faith is orn down and my hope is crushed, then where is it possible to flee?" His question echoed verse one, where he determined to take refuge in the Lord. f my faith is weakened, my heart breaking and my hope diminishing, vhat hope do I have but to run back to God?"

In verses four and five, David gave us a reason for that hope. "The Lord s in his holy temple; the Lord's throne is in heaven; his eyes see, his eyelids est the children of man. The Lord tests the righteous, but his soul hates he wicked and the one who loves violence" (Psalm 11:4-5). In this passage, ve see God's response to two kinds of people. One type of person is tested vhile the other type is terrified. Why terrified? Because God's "soul hates the wicked." This is a fearful thing for evildoers to consider. Meanwhile, God's people are tested by the arrows fired at them in the dark. Of what value are these tests? Our enemies mean them to break us, but God uses them to prove His protection and power. Our tests teach us how to run through troops and leap over walls (see Psalm 18:29). David wanted us to know that God will test us but not so that we fail. Our test will be one that leads to victory. Our tests also reveal God's power, and that terrifies our enemies. David gave us the reason they should fear. "Let him rain coals on the wicked; fire and sulfur and a scorching wind shall be the portion of their cup" (Psalm 11:6).

I am awed as I consider the tests that my professor endured and the victory that God gave him. It is heartbreaking to think of any child being tested as severely as my professor was at his tender age. I'm not suggesting that God brought those tests on him; I only mean that the tests that befell him led to something glorious. Today, my professor has a ministry of national and international reach to help people who have been sexually abused, touching thousands with healing and restoration. His own story demonstrates the unlimited power of God's loving grace to redeem and transform any life, no matter how damaged. We can flee to Him, because He sees all that we go through. "The Lord is in his holy temple; the Lord's throne is in heaven; his eyes see . . . " (Psalm 11:4). God is sovereign, omnipotent, and unchanging, and that means His refuge is a foundational security to us.

Those who are not being tested, the wicked and ungodly, become terrified. They will not triumph but instead will see their works overturned Hot coals of conviction will rain down on their heads, and their lot will be scorching destruction. "Let him rain coals on the wicked; fire and sulfur and a scorching wind shall be the portion of their cup" (Psalm 11:5-6). This is God's judgment, plain and simple; and it will come upon the wicked rapidly ke a wildfire, consuming their corrupted lives. They may have triumphed for a short season, but their ending is pain, sorrow and self-loathing. That is the cup of judgment they have to drink unless they turn and repent.

The lives of the upright are a different story. "For the Lord is righteous; he loves righteous deeds; the upright shall behold his face" (Psalm 11:7). When I consider my grandmother and professor, I see people who have gone through dark times and were shown the light of God's face. They emerged triumphant, entering the victory that the Lord had for them. They did not let their test defeat them. When they needed help, they ran to the refuge of God's presence, which renewed their strength. It was not apparent to the naked eye, but over time my grandmother and professor were each granted unlimited power over the arrows that were fired at them. In the end, both passed their tests with flying colors.

You and I have been promised the power to pass our tests too. We can face our season of darkness and time of trouble as arrows fly at us from all directions. At times we'll be alarmed by everything that comes at us, causing us to wonder, "Why am I in this place? I can't handle all of this at one time. Whenever I pray for relief, more arrows fly at me." No matter how dark the night and how fiercely the arrows fly, God has His hand over your life. He has a purpose for you, and your testing will bring you out of the darkness and into greater glory to Him and joy to your soul. When you refuse to give up, turning to Him at your most difficult time, you accomplish more for His kingdom than ever.

In those times, we find ourselves encompassed by God's protecting hand. He points and says, "See My servant in the midst of the dark. That arrow flew at her, but she stood strong. She had faith, and she fled to me to draw on my strength. She shall see my face." That ultimately is what the psalmist desired. He knew that by taking refuge in the Lord he could endure the long, dark nights in the difficult seasons as arrows flew. Later in the psalter we read that spending one day in God's house is better than 1,000 days anywhere else (see Psalm 84:10). Just to see the light of the Lord's countenance carried him. The same holds true for us.

Wherever you find yourself today, whether triumphing over difficulties or in the midst of a test, you can fly away to the high place God has made for you in His presence, away from all fear and despondency and into His holy temple where His unlimited power is available to you. Psalm 91 declares, "You will not fear the terror of the night, nor the arrow that flies by day, nor the pestilence that stalks in darkness, nor the destruction that wastes at noonday" (Psalm 91:5-6). When you have endured your test, you will see His face.

No matter what test you are enduring, no matter what dark valley you find yourself in, you will not fall. Seek His refuge, and your reward will be His countenance, its light piercing the darkness you have just been through. To all who suffer and despair, His joy will come; His hope will sustain, and His grace will cover and carry you. You will emerge from the dark with the strength of victory to His great glory.

CHAPTER THIRTEEN

Psalm 12
Born Into a Battle

1 Save, O Lord, for the godly one is gone;

    for the faithful have vanished from among the children of man.

2 Everyone utters lies to his neighbor;

    with flattering lips and a double heart they speak.

3 May the Lord cut off all flattering lips,

    the tongue that makes great boasts,

4 those who say, "With our tongue we will prevail,

    our lips are with us; who is master over us?"

5 "Because the poor are plundered, because the needy groan,

    I will now arise," says the Lord;

    "I will place him in the safety for which he longs."

6 The words of the Lord are pure words,

    like silver refined in a furnace on the ground,

    purified seven times.

7 You, O Lord, will keep them;

    you will guard us from this generation forever.

8 On every side the wicked prowl,

    as vileness is exalted among the children of man.

ONE OF THE MAJOR REALITIES we've seen reflected in the psalms so far is one of warfare. The initial group of psalms laid out the conflict taking place between people under the sway of evil and those who are righteous. It is clear this is not a one-time conflict nor does it happen sporadically. We have to understand we are born into a battle.

I believe that Christians who are most depressed, discouraged, and ready to give up in life fall into one of two categories. They are either uncertain about whether God answers prayer, or they believe they should not be living with conflicts. If we understand that we are born into war, we'll accept that we're going to face conflicts. This includes hardship, suffering, pain, loss, grief, and battles. Along with conflicts, however, we are going to see great victories. All told, the psalmists want you to understand very clearly that you are in a fight.

When I was in high school, I was threatened by a bully. At the time I was taking lessons in kung fu and kickboxing. When the bully said he wanted to fight, I answered, "I'm a Christian, so I don't want to fight you," but like any bully, he came after me anyway. With my little bit of training I knew how to duck-and-roll out of harm's way when he attacked. I also knew how to throw a jab. The bully threw wild, roundhouse haymakers at me, but I was able to dodge him and back him off without being hit. In a short while, he got winded; he also got jabbed a few times. In the end he got frustrated and gave up.

You may not want to be in a battle or a fight. You may want to live in comfort and ease, going to church without worries and seeing God's promises fulfilled without struggles. The truth is that you're going to be confronted by worrisome thoughts, by evil, and by the temptation of your own flesh. The psalms prepare us for all of this. By the time we come to Psalm 12, we see that the psalmist was very focused on a motif of warfare.

l of us will face people who oppose us, but the psalmist's focus here was
n internal conflicts as well as external ones. One important theme of this
salm is that we can be set free from internal conflicts, a deliverance that
n help us when exterior enemies come against us. In short, this is all
out the warfare of godly people.

As Psalm 12 opens, David spoke of how the hearts of righteous people
ave been influenced by the wicked. "Save, O Lord, for the godly one is
one; for the faithful have vanished from among the children of man.
veryone utters lies to his neighbor; with flattering lips and a double heart
ey speak" (Psalm 12:1-2). What caused the godly to fall away and into
icked practices like these? One way is that the enemy can put words in
ur ears that cause us to be anxious, fearful, depressed, and discouraged.
his can lead to temptation to find sources of comfort and direction other
an the Lord. David addressed this in the next verse. "May the Lord cut
ff all flattering lips, the tongue that makes great boasts" (Psalm 12:3).
e was speaking of an attitude of heart that culminates in an arrogance
oward God. "Those who say, 'With our tongue we will prevail, our lips
re with us; who is master over us?'" (Psalm 12:4). In other words, "We're
n charge. Everything is under our control, and nothing can stop us."

Satan tries to deceive even faithful Christians with the lie that the
wicked will prevail. This includes everything from hardships to relational
onflicts to sinful habits. He wants to convince you these things will
lways be your master. David spoke to this condition in verse five.
Because the poor are plundered, because the needy groan" (Psalm 12:5).
Do you ever feel plundered? Do you struggle under what feels like the
elentless grip of financial troubles or relational strife, things that drain
ou of the abundant life God promised? Maybe you ask yourself from
ime to time, "Is this the way life is supposed to be? Is this how marriage

should look? Is this how my work life should be going?" These are among the groans of the needy whom David referenced. Consider what the Lord said about it. "'Because the poor are plundered, because the needy groan, I will now arise,' says the Lord. 'I will place him in the safety for which he longs'" (Psalm 12:7). The Lord will come to the rescue of the righteous.

The rest of the psalm addresses a cultural warfare, a battle between good and evil, between wickedness and righteousness, between people who mock God and those who follow Him. "The words of the Lord are pure words, like silver refined in a furnace on the ground, purified seven times. You, O Lord, will keep them; you will guard us from this generation forever. On every side the wicked prowl, as vileness is exalted among the children of man" (Psalm 12:6-8). At times we are tempted to believe the lies that the enemy whispers in our ear, lies that are designed to undermine our faith. These can be aimed at us by earthly opponents, but at the same time warfare is happening in the spiritual realm between demonic forces and the power of heaven. As I write this, a culture war is certainly taking place in the nations, as rampant wickedness increases with almost no boundaries. However, there is an even greater war taking place, one that's more daunting, and it takes place in unseen realms. This war is happening whether we like it or not, and it confronts us with a question: Will we allow the Holy Spirit to fill us with His might and strength to face this conflict? Will we stand up against the vileness that is being exalted and recognize that the opponent we battle is Satan?

To respond properly to this question, I find it helpful to work backward through the psalm. Verse eight says, "On every side the wicked prowl, as vileness is exalted among the children of man" (Psalm 12:8). Forces of evil are at work against us. They oppose the church and entire nations. They also work against the wellbeing of our family, health, mental state, nd most especially our spiritual life. When we read that "on every side he wicked prowl," the image is of Satan, of whom John says, "The thief comes only to steal and kill and destroy" (John 10:10). Today we see Satan prowling through our culture and institutions, exalting vile practices that only a few years ago were socially unacceptable. Dark things done in secret are now boasted about in public, "the tongue that makes great boasts" (Psalm 12:3).

We see this boasting tongue in the media, in government, and in our educational system. Cultural practices that fifty years ago would have been considered abhorrent are now acted out with neither shame nor restraint but with boasting. Sadly, I see this in the church as well. For decades, the liberal church opened its doors to practices that cause the godly to anguish. Now similar practices are creeping into the evangelical church, with the Word of God being compromised. Certain behaviors once seen as outlandish, foolish, and even outright abominations are tolerated. The apostle Paul had to deal with this in the church at Corinth. A young man in the congregation was sleeping with his stepmother, and church leaders weren't bringing correction. What was happening in that church called for more than correction, however; it involved spiritual warfare. To contend for the faith, Paul demanded church discipline and at the same time pointed out the prevalent cultural norms spreading through the church.

In addition to attacks on the church are attacks on our person. Satan prowls on every side of your life, from your marriage to your health to your emotions to your spiritual wellbeing. He comes to attack all of it. When you wake up in the morning under a cloud of depression and don't know why you feel so discouraged, you can know Satan is prowling to take advantage. The source of your depression may be physiological rather than spiritual, but the powers of darkness use it to align against you and boast in your ear that you are worthless. This is how the warfare we face enters into our personal life.

David addressed what should we do when we find ourselves in a battle with the culture. However, what was David's desire as he found himself in warfare over his broken family, his crushing emotions and his desolate future? How did he ask the Lord to deal with it all? In verse seven, he spoke for all of us who face warfare from the surrounding culture and from our own personal anguish. "You, O Lord, will keep them; you will guard us from this generation forever" (Psalm 12:7). This is a powerful word for a generation under warfare. Does it often seem to you as if the wicked prevail, that God is moving too slowly or not at all, or that evil is advancing too rapidly? Does it sometimes feel as if the forces of darkness are stronger than the power of God's light? David responded, in essence, "Lord, guard us from that feeling of 'defeat.' Let us not be overcome by it. Your Word and Your promises are true. Guard our minds so that we won't believe the lies Satan throws at us and instead believe You will keep us."

Still, at times perhaps you feel hopeless. Maybe you feel ready to give up because your prayers seem to have no effect against the tide of wickedness rolling over you. Maybe you've accepted that this is the reality of the world and there's nothing you can do about it. Or maybe you've "spiritualized" what's happening, thinking, "God is sovereign, so maybe He wants these forces to prevail for some reason unknown to me."

The Lord does not need evil to prevail for you to gain spiritual strength. He is not a God Who sits by while evil defeats those who love Him. He is a breakthrough God. Whatever you're facing and no matter how long the season of struggle has lasted, He wants you trained for warfare. He wants you equipped so as wickedness rises like a tumultuous flood, your faith is raised higher. Certainly, at times He sends a wind from heaven to blow away

ellish forces in a rebuke to the enemy, but His way is almost always to use
s to do battle. He is Lord over all, and He uses chosen vessels to come against
1e powers of darkness in order to destroy their works. God wants you to be
1at kind of person. To ensure it, He promises to guard and keep you.

How do we get to such a place of trust as wickedness prowls around us?
1oes God give us instructions on how to enlarge our capacity to win these
attles? Verse six holds a powerfully instructive truth. "The words of the
ord are pure words, like silver refined in a furnace on the ground, purified
even times" (Psalm 12:6). God doesn't speak words with doublemindedness
ut with force. This contrasts directly with the seductive deceptions of
attering human beings. "With flattering lips and a double heart they
peak" (Psalm 12:2). Unlike flattery, God's word is wholeheartedly pure.
Moreover, once God says something, it is as good as done. You may not see
he full fruition of His word immediately, but you will eventually in His
iming. His word cannot fail.

Three New Testament passages speak to the warfare that every
eneration faces despite Jesus' authority over all things. The following
passages declare that Christ has total authority with all things sitting
ubject under His feet." Even so, Paul explained why not everything is
ompletely subject under Christ's authority as yet. "Then comes the end,
when he delivers the kingdom to God the Father after destroying every
ule and every authority and power. For he must reign until he has put
ill his enemies under his feet. The last enemy to be destroyed is death.
'or 'God has put all things in subjection under his feet.' But when it says,
ill things are put in subjection,' it is plain that he is excepted who put all
hings in subjection under him. When all things are subjected to him,
hen the Son himself will also be subjected to him who put all things in
ubjection under him, that God may be all in all" (1 Corinthians 15:24-28).

According to Paul, Jesus is destroying the works of Satan. This work is continuous, and He calls you and me to participate in it. Paul added in Ephesians, "And he put all things under his feet and gave him as head over all things to the church, which is his body, the fullness of him who fills all in all" (Ephesians 1:22-23).

Finally, consider this moving passage from Hebrews, which testifies to our participation in Christ's work against evil and to the reward we are promised.

> For it was not to angels that God subjected the world to come, of which we are speaking. It has been testified somewhere, 'What is man, that you are mindful of him, or the son of man, that you care for him? You made him for a little while lower than the angels; you have crowned him with glory and honor, putting everything in subjection under his feet.' Now in putting everything in subjection to him, he left nothing outside his control. At present, we do not yet see everything in subjection to him. But we see him who for a little while was made lower than the angels, namely Jesus, crowned with glory and honor because of the suffering of death, so that by the grace of God he might taste death for everyone. For it was fitting that he, for whom and by whom all things exist, in bringing many sons to glory, should make the founder of their salvation perfect through suffering. For he who sanctifies and those who are sanctified all have one source. That is why he is not ashamed to call them brothers, saying, 'I will tell of your name to my brothers; in the midst of the congregation I will sing your praise' (Hebrews 2:5-12).

Even Old Testament passages speak prophetically to Christ's authority including one we have read previously in Psalm 8. "You have given him dominion over the works of your hands; you have put all things under his feet" (Psalm 8:6). Clearly, Jesus has been given dominion over all things

ur role with Him is essentially the cleanup process over the devil's final
sidue of death.

God said He promises to raise us up for this work. Once we accept His
ernal word as true, faith begins to rise up in us, building an expectation.
'e no longer wake up each morning believing the new day will be like
'ery other day, full of difficulty and defeat. Instead, we have faith to say,
ven though my circumstances haven't changed, my heart is changing. I
ave faith and listen to the voice of the Father, Who speaks good things."
'e trust that we can triumph over any trial because nothing is too hard for
he Lord. We sense He has a purpose and plan for us, and so we say with
aul, "I can do all things through him who strengthens me" (Philippians
13). We believe God yeah,will accomplish through us all He sends us forth
o do.

We live in a generation in which wickedness prowls and vileness
i exalted, yet it is also a generation in which God's promises endure as
ure with power for victory. When Satan attacks, the purity of God's
'ord rises up in us giving us boldness to resist. Otherwise, we may be
empted to wonder, "Is God really good? Can His word be trusted?" This
i what happened in the Garden of Eden. Satan planted doubts in Adam
nd Eve when he asked, "Did God really say not to eat this fruit? Could he
e withholding something from you?" (Genesis 3:1). It is a tragic thing to
isten to the wrong voice instead of to God's.

The Lord steps in on our behalf. "'Because the poor are plundered,
ecause the needy groan, I will now arise,' says the Lord; 'I will place him
n the safety for which he longs'" (Psalm 12:5). In spiritual terms, we are the
oor and needy in this verse. We have to recognize our spiritual bankruptcy,
ur warfare deficiency and the ineffectiveness of our faith. The word for
lundered" in this verse suggests being taken down or pulled away. I picture

a vulnerable person holding a bag full of coins as a robber reaches in and take most of the money. However, many of us don't recognize when we've bee plundered. We have a false sense of confidence, claiming that everything i fine when it's not. In this respect, we agree with the devil's word rather tha with God's. Isaiah speaks of the Lord coming "to comfort all who mour to grant to those who mourn in Zion—to give them a beautiful headdres instead of ashes, the oil of gladness instead of mourning, the garment o praise instead of a faint spirit; that they may be called oaks of righteousnes the planting of the Lord, that he may be glorified" (Isaiah 61:2-3).

We must be able to mourn our condition before we can be comfortec The "safety" to which God carries us is what we think of as deliverance He stops the robbing hand of the wicked prowler and guards us. For thi to happen, we must agree with God's Word rather than the enemy's.

Some people have been so plundered that they've given up all thei longings and desires. They no longer believe that the Lord has grea things for them ahead. When they hear sermons about God's plans fo us, they scoff. They hear worship songs about the Lord being victor anc think, "Really? Why wasn't He victor when things fell apart in my life?"

So many things fell apart for David. As he groaned, faith arose ir his heart. " . . . because the needy groan, I will now arise,' says the Lord (Psalm 12:5). Afterward, David testified, "You, O Lord, will keep them; you will guard us from this generation forever" (Psalm 12:7).

Verses two through four describe the people of a wicked culture the hellish forces who drive them and the personal conflicts we each battle within. "Everyone utters lies to his neighbor; with flattering lips and a double heart they speak. May the Lord cut off all flattering lips the tongue that makes great boasts, those who say, 'With our tongue we will prevail, our lips are with us; who is master over us?'" (Psalm 12:2-4)

Whether this describes a national culture or personal attacks, it speaks of vileness being exalted. The enemy boasts, "I'm going to speak lies, and no one can stop me. I'm so skilled in this dark art that no one is master over me, not even the faithfulness of God or the purity of His word. So I will boast about how I can plunder and prevail over any Christian."

When we hear lies from this voice, they may make sense at first. This can lead us into making agreements with the devil's word rather than the Lord's. Many of us fell victim to this in childhood as we absorbed damaging words from the people around us. "You can't do anything right. Nobody wants you around. You're worthless to everyone. You're ugly. You're fat. You're stupid. You're unwanted." These voices, buried deep inside us, remain with us into adulthood and influence our spiritual life. We believe their lies because we see some element of truth in them. Moses faced this dilemma as God called him to lead the Israelites out of Egypt. He immediately doubted, thinking, "I can't do that. I am slow of speech. How can I possibly lead people if I can't communicate with them?" In his mind, he limited what God could do through him because he thought nothing good could happen due to his stutter. Moses had to free himself from that lie. He had to hear the word that God would be with him.

It is one thing to believe the enemy's lie ("You're no good"); it's another to live out the results of that lie ("It's true. I really am no good"). The enemy makes a deep connection between his deceptions and the core of our heart. The times comes, however, when God reveals His precious promises to us, and we are given power to overcome the lies Satan has planted in us.

Do you attach more confidence to the enemy's words about you than to God's? To prevent ourselves from being plundered further, we need to groan out our pain and seek the Lord to break through for us. We need to simply pray, "Lord, I choose to break all these agreements

I have made with the enemy's lies. Even if there is some truth to what I hear, Your word about me is supreme truth. It will not let lies affect my outcome."

The book of Revelation said this is how we overcome lies and experience deliverance. "And they have conquered him by the blood of the Lamb and by the word of their testimony" (Revelation 12:11).

Three simple practices free us from the agreements we have made with the enemy's lies. The first spiritual practice to use is our testimony. We claim, "I believe I can do all things through Christ. Even if I stutter there is no hindrance to how God can use me. He can heal me, but even if He doesn't, He can use my weakness to His glory. Every accusation about me has been nailed to the cross of Christ, and I no longer believe them. I know the enemy will cast them at me again, but I will plead the blood of Jesus, whose victory is total."

Second, God has created us to be in a community of love. We can love and receive love, and that is a different way of living than enduring the lies that cripple us. Rather than living in defeat, our walk in Christ's love transforms the world around us.

Third, we lay down our lives in obedience to Jesus, stating, "Lord, my life is not my own. Make me a living sacrifice for You and Your glory. By Your empowering grace, I will not live in compromise, lukewarmness, or half-heartedness. Let Your promises release in me the power to accomplish Your purposes."

Having worked backward in this psalm from verse eight ("On every side the wicked prowl"), we arrive at David's plea in verse one ("Save, O Lord, for the godly one is gone"). David had a sense of what needed to happen. He prayed, in essence, "Lord, You have to save me from this situation, from these wicked prowlers and their lies that plague me with

oughts of defeat. Help me to see fully the testimony You have given
e and to stand in Your power for my life." When you are in agreement
ith God's Word, your life is transformed by it. Those who oppose you
om the dark culture will see God's glory at work in you, and His Spirit
ill confront them with pure truth. His Word has been tested through
illennia and stands pure and unchangeable. This, in short, is the
arfare we wage. As for the battle itself, His enduring Word tells us, "No,
all these things we are more than conquerors through him who loved
s" (Romans 8:37).

Scripture Index

Subject Index

use 12, 22, 78, 91, 96, 115-116, 122, 139, 147, 159, 163, 172-174, 176

diction 42, 44-45, 54, 149, 152, 161, 165

ager

God's 84, 88, 90-92, 94-95, 97

holy 66-67

human 21, 26, 45, 48, 87

of Satan 138

of the nations 12, 16, 25, 27, 29, 31-32, 34, 40, 59, 112, 129, 136

nxiety 69, 74, 136, 143

rrogance

See pride

tonement 91, 96-97

itterness 21-22, 106

lessing 13, 53, 63-64, 80, 82, 112, 130, 140, 150

ondage 30-31, 64

essationism 101-102, *See also* false doctrine

chaos 26, 28-29, 31, 37, 40, 64

character of God 10, 32, 34, 72, 103, 118, 123-124

children 17, 28, 43, 78, 137-138, 172-173

Christ, Jesus 13, 17, 19-20, 22, 29, 30-31, 33, 41, 51-52, 55, 59, 64-66, 82, 91, 93-96, 103-107, 109-110, 121, 124-125, 138-139, 141-143, 167, 185-186, 190

Chrysostom, John 58

cleansing 81, 120-121, 137, 156

cross, the 20, 30, 31, 55, 90-91, 93, 95, 97, 104, 141, 143, 152, 167, 190

culture (worldly) 15, 22, 26, 30, 64, 67, 115, 183, 188

curse 96, 97, 157, 159

D

death 18-20, 31, 62, 78, 83-85, 87-88, 90, 93, 96, 99-101, 141-142, 146, 151-153, 155, 167, 185-187

deception 21, 27, 31, 141, 185, 189

deliverance 40, 49, 51, 83-84, 86-87, 101, 103, 105, 129, 136, 148-150, 152-153, 155, 166, 173, 181, 188, 190

Biography

GARY WILKERSON IS THE PRESIDENT of World Challenge, an international mission organization that was founded by his father, David Wilkerson. He has traveled nationally and internationally at conferences and conducted mission ventures such as church planting, starting orphanages, clinics, feeding programs among the poorest of the poor and the most unreached people of the earth.

A CrossFit enthusiast, Gary often hikes the Rocky Mountains' breathtaking front range in Colorado. He and his wife, Kelly, live in Colorado Springs with their four children and ten grandchildren.

This book is published in association with World Challenge.

Transforming lives through the message and mission of Jesus Christ

For more information about
WORLD CHALLENGE
and
The Altar of Our Hearts
please visit:

www.worldchallenge.org

Ambassador International's mission is to magnify the Lord Jesus Christ and promote His Gospel through the written word.

We believe through the publication of Christian literature, Jesus Christ and His Word will be exalted, believers will be strengthened in their walk with Him, and the lost will be directed to Jesus Christ as the only way of salvation.

For more information about
AMBASSADOR INTERNATIONAL
please visit:

www.ambassador-international.com
@AmbassadorIntl
www.facebook.com/AmbassadorIntl

Ambassador International
GREENVILLE, SOUTH CAROLINA & BELFAST, NORTHERN IRELAND

www.ambassador-international.com
Magnifying Jesus while promoting His gospel through the written word.

More from Ambassador International...

Most of us know Who Jesus is and would admit that He was a good and kind Teacher while here on earth. But He is so much more—He is our Savior and God and worthy of all our worship. Through an in-depth study into the book of Hebrews, Joshua West and Gary Wilkerson take apart each verse, drawing the reader to a closer look at the Man Who lived here on earth for a short time. If you are searching for something more from God, dive into this study and drink in the jaw-dropping beauty of our Jesus.

Many readers of the Bible assume that when Jesus did a miracle it was, fundamentally, to prove that He was God—Jesus was pulling out His "God Card." What if Jesus was intending to reveal something different, something more, something beyond merely proving His identity? Seeing as Jesus' miracles were such a significant part of His ministry, if we miss what His miracles do reveal, we may be missing out on great insights into the One Who loves us and came to rescue us. You will never read about the miracles in the same way . . . and you will catch a renewed and compelling glimpse of Jesus.

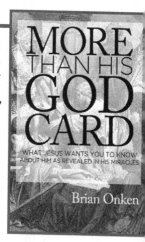

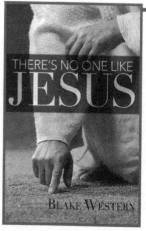

Readers will develop a deep love and gain perspective into Jesus by His Word, His miracles, His salvation, His friendship and much more as Blake Western reveals the absolute power and majesty of Jesus. Western offers keen understanding into why no one can compare to Jesus as the King of kings and Lord of lords. Unveiling Jesus in this way makes for an excellent read that will overflow many hearts with love for our Savior and also reminds all that Jesus is the anchor to our souls and the answer to everything you will ever need in this life.

Made in the USA
Columbia, SC
21 June 2024

37079781R00115